Stripped for Greater:

Walk by Faith

By Michele Nicole

For we walk by faith and not by sight.

2 Corinthians 5:7 (KJV)

I wonder when we call ourselves "believers" do we really understand the price that has been paid for our faith walk?

I wonder if we really understand the psychological agony and emotional upheaval that occurs when we are called into this walk of faith.

We must count up the cost.

This book is dedicated to those who walk with God and have the scars to prove it.

Michele Nicole

"I'm gonna tell you a story, which comes from the pages, that make up the book of *MY* life."   - Michele Nicole

WHAT WAS SAID

"There comes a time when you must perform an adult critique of your life, where you will ask yourself, at what point do I stop existing and start living." -Bishop George Bloomer

"You must learn to trust God, even when you cannot trace God."- Pastor Philip Anthony Mitchell

"When you a have purpose for your life, it disciplines your behavior and chooses your habits." –Dr. Myles Munroe

"You can either live a life of preventive maintenance or a life of damage control."- Clarence Harding

"Grace on my life for what I am dealing with right now. It doesn't mean I like it, it doesn't mean I want it, it doesn't mean I enjoy it, it just means that, whatever this is, whatever I am dealing with, it will not kill me."- Bishop TD Jakes

"If you don't deal with the cause of a problem, dealing with the behavior that comes because of the problem is a waste of time." –Tony Robbins

"Practice till you get it right, then practice some more till you can't get it wrong."- Dharyl Anton

"You made a lot of plans for your life, but did you ask God what His plans are for your life?" – Leo Lawrence Mitchell

"You do not have to put yourself through pain in order for you to learn the lesson."-Ian McFall

"Humility and acceptance brings a strength that arrogance and pride can never give."- Michael McFall

"God isn't at work producing the circumstances you want, God is at work in bad circumstances producing the you that He wants."- John Ortberg

"I consider that our present sufferings are not worth comparing with the glory that will be revealed in us."- Roman 8:18 (NIV)

Table of Contents:

The days that became weeks

July 2016

Sunday	Monday	Tuesday	Wednesday	Thursday	Friday	Saturday
					1	2
3	4	5	6	7	8	9
10	11	12	13	14	15	16
17	18	19	20	21	22	23
24	25	26	27	28	29	30
31						

© www.calendarpedia.com   4: Independence Day   Data provided 'as is' without warranty

August 2016

Sunday	Monday	Tuesday	Wednesday	Thursday	Friday	Saturday
	1	2	3	4	5	6
7	8	9	10	11	12	13
14	15	16	17	18	19	20
21	22	23	24	25	26	27
28	29	30	31			

© www.calendarpedia.com   Data provided 'as is' without warranty

September 2016

Sunday	Monday	Tuesday	Wednesday	Thursday	Friday	Saturday
				1	2	3
4	5	6	7	8	9	10
11	12	13	14	15	16	17
18	19	20	21	22	23	24
25	26	27	28	29	30	

OH
MY
GOD

Monday July 11th, 2016

The apartment is mine no longer.

I am standing inside the apartment in front of the living room window looking out at the view. The tree outside is sturdy and strong. The leaves wave at me as if to say goodbye. I turned to the left and then the right. The apartment was bare. No pictures on the walls nor any memories of moments of laughter or achievements proudly being displayed. Turning and facing into the apartment, I see only the items that are too big to take with me as I prepare to leave. I completed my final walk throughout the apartment. I paused and looked for anything that should leave with me. It was time. The closing and locking of the door was the loudest thing I did in the silence. The stroll to the car was deliberately slow. The engine turned over and I shifted the car into drive. Heading to the property manager's office, I was numbed. Actually, I was on automatic pilot.

I placed the key in the property manager's hand and thanked her for everything. It's July and I'm in Atlanta. It's hot as hell in Atlanta in July!

The car was waiting for me. He was the silent friend that was always there. His presence let me know that I knew better and that the situation could have been avoided had I simply obeyed the instructions that

2

were given. On the back seat, there was a garment bag with clothing items, a plastic grocery bag with food items, another bag with toiletries, and a trunk of trinkets and "just in-case" items.

I had $0.06 in my bank account and $5 in coins in my purse. As I sat in the car, the reality of this season of my life just hit me...homeless. I am homeless.

I looked at myself in the mirror and the conversation in my mind began. "It's all your fault. You did this to me. Yes, you failed us. You are forty-six years old and you have nothing. You are stuck. You are in "starting over" mode once again. You are not all here, you are "functioning broken." You once had a full-time job with great benefits and ran a traveling business as well. You were almost done paying down your debts and you had begun to make plans for the next season of your life. How did you go from that to now sitting in your car with $.06 in the bank and $5 in your purse? How did you go from having a place to stay to now having to put all of your items in storage and packed clothes laying on the back seat? You have two college degrees but you're only making $8.50 per hour working part time. How the fuck did this happen to us Michele? Please tell me because I would like to know."

"We in survivor mode now. What did you do? Damn! This is some fucked up shit I gotta clean up as usual. I ain't hearing shit you gotta say so sit yo ass down and let me figure this thing out!" I said to myself.

It is the gorilla side of me. It is the part that always presents itself to protect the weaker 6-year-old. The 6-year-old could not argue with the gorilla side of me. She was in a corner of my mind curled up and crying, in need of being rescued.

Looking in the mirror, I cannot see myself. Looking past the mirror, I cannot see anything at all. (Sigh) What am I going to do now? What do I do now? Wait! My mom was getting ready to relocate and this would be her final week. She was packing her items and would be in need of help. It made sense. I made the call and she said of course I could swing by and help. Should I tell her about my current situation? Should I tell anyone about my situation? No, No! I will not!

Deep within me, in a place where human hands cannot touch and reason and logic have no influence, I had a notion. It was one that could not be explained but it must be trusted without understanding. This was the beginning of something that will be greater than I could grasp at this current time. This was the beginning of a process. The name of the process would be revealed later.

Heading over to my mom's house was bittersweet. Goodbye to my own house and soon to be goodbye to my mom. My grandmother used to say, "These are the changing scenes of life."

I wonder what will the next scene be like?

Tuesday July 12th - Friday July 15th

The house was constantly buzzing with my family, friends from church, and neighborhood folks as they came and went.

Many hands lightened the load and there were lots of, "taking this" and, "don't need that" and, "put it in that pile" and, "Oh my God, that picture is so old" and, "yyyoooooo, I remember that moment" and, "That's Buffa, the family pet who was the smartest dog that ever lived." When items that belonged to my father were discovered, there would be a silent pause along with moments of reflection.

He is in heaven now. Hey Papa Leo.

I stayed the week and helped my mama pack. I had a roof over my head, a place to take a hot shower and eat a good meal, sleep in a warm bed, reminisce and enjoyed some grown-folk conversation. During the afternoons, I got dressed and went to work and took care of my responsibility. After work, I returned to my mom's house and enjoyed the moments. When she would mention the amount of time I was spending away from my apartment, I became dismissive and immediately went into cover up mode.

We attached the VCR player to the TV and watched old family movies and other old movies in general. Some of the tapes were so old that they got stuck in the player and required more than yanking and pulling to remove them. As mom made us some home cooking, we laughed at old hair styles, school-days clothes, talked about the old neighborhood, looked at pictures of the nieces and nephews when they were younger and smiled at pictures of family members that were long gone. This week was truly one that was most enjoyable.

I was around the people I truly loved.

Saturday July 16th

Today was the day my mom and sister would be making the drive to her future in another state.

I hugged, kissed, prayed and appreciated them both. It was hard to see mom go, but after all, she had sacrificed for the family. It was her time for self.

Time for work. In the rearview mirror, the house where we had congregated over the past few days grew further away. Looking through the windshield, my job got closer. Looking at the clock on my dashboard, time kept on ticking and looking into my mind, the reality of homelessness started to set in. I was working at a local retail clothing store. I was grateful for the job but disappointed in myself. There were comings and goings, conversations and laughter, directing and assisting. It was the distraction that I needed, but it would not last long. It was time for the store to close. As the managers locked up the store, some of us gathered around our car and talked.

This car, a 1997 Infinity I-30 with over 230,000 miles, was now so much more. It was now my mobile home. I am one of many people who live or have lived out of their car. As my co-workers prepared to leave, I heard them joking and laughing, "Man, bruh, I can't wait to get home." Hearing that was a punch in my guts hard and viciously in a most innocent way.

"Well Michele, this is your home. Now where are we to go?" I said to myself.

Starting the car, I sat still. Then it was time to drive. I drove to the house that now sat empty. The house where my mom used to live. It was quiet and still. The neighborhood was quiet and still. I rolled up slowly and parked a couple of houses down and then decided to park in front the house. As I settled in, there was a blanket, a pillow and sheet in the back seat. There was a presence in my mind to keep these things handy, now I knew why. I changed into an old t-shirt and light jogging pants. My work clothes were folded and placed into a suitcase in the trunk and the dirty items were placed in a black plastic bag.

In the silence of night, I began to have the conversation with myself that was long overdue.

"You know, it does not have to be like this Michele. You can get help from the family, and you can even get help from your Church if you ask," I thought to myself.

That thought was probably right, but it did not feel right. I had a strong aversion to asking and accepting help for this particular situation. It felt like I would be aborting something that was attached to my moment of failure. My downfall was because of disobedience, but it is disobedience and something deeper. This specific...episode is bigger than I understand. No. Helping hands would abort the birth. Helping hands will make the process last longer. There is a bigger plan. I must trust the process.

Was I punishing myself? Why did it feel like I was punishing myself? Am I punishing myself because—? Truth is, I was punishing myself to make sure that the lesson would sink in. I wanted to finally get it, correct it, understand it, receive it, surrender to it, and eventually change it. The only problem is I did not know what the "IT" was.

I made the choices and decisions that led me to being here. I wanted this experience, this specific time of hardship. This is the pity party side of me. This is the "poor me", "woe is me", "I can't seem to get it right" party I attend. Yet I feel that there is something more. There is something that is not connecting. Am I operating out of a malfunctioning thought pattern? Why do I keep putting forth efforts when no results are being yielded? Am I brain-damaged? Is my deductive reason and logic damaged? Something is wrong! How do I fix it? What are the short circuits that continuously bring these types of extreme outcomes? I am a grown ass woman and I can't make a sound decision? I can't take care of myself? What is the problem with me?

The problem is I am "functioning broken." I am in a state of "functioning broken" and I need help. I cracked the window enough for a breeze to find its way into the car and nothing or no one else. As I lay on my side, my ears became my eyes. They were extremely sensitive. I was on high alert for my life. My gorilla was trained on the streets of New York and she was not one to fuck with.

I listened for the slightest movement, footstep, crack of a branch or twig, laughter from a house, a car driving by, anything and everything. It is CODE RED all night. I went back and forth from dozing to jumping up. After each jump, I looked around and then laid in the back seat and drifted off to sleep.

My biggest fear is that I would open my eyes and see a curious face or a couple of strange sadistic faces with hungry eyes and undisciplined behavior that would attempt to open the car door. I have something for such an attempt. I keep protection on me at all times.

I have not always been saved.

THIS SEASONS NECESSITIES

Sunday July 17th

I made it through the first night.

As I sat up on the back seat, I looked around the neighborhood, no strange faces outside my car window, no one grasping at my door, nothing. There was nothing but silence. It was 5:02 am. The earth was still, the dew was on the grass, and I am alive.

"Good morning God. Good morning Jesus. Good morning Holy Spirit. Good morning Angels that the Lord has given charge over me. This is the day that the Lord has made, I will rejoice and be glad in it," I said.

Morning responsibilities are calling my name. It's Sunday, where am I going? I drove around a section of town where it is busy. I wanted to see the prices for hotels on this side of town. I made lefts and rights, another right some more lefts, up a hill and then towards the back of a street. I was finally there.

I did not know this place was here. As I made my way into the lobby there is a young lady who answered my questions about prices and safety and amenities. We took a look at the different rooms. Something in my Spirit was not right. We went back to the lobby and began to talk.

The conversation began with her agitation with God, her current home situation, her being stuck, her frustrations, uncertainties, lack of confidence, losing hope and struggling with faith. As she spoke, I asked the Lord for help. How am I, a woman who is functioning broken, supposed to help her make it through and hold on for one more day? "My sister, do you not know that in moments like this, in a crisis like this, in times like these, when everything has been taken, now more than ever we are called to trust God even when we can't trace God?". The tears were flowing. It was what she needed to hear and with that moment of accepting what was said, the Holy Spirit began to minister to her in depths only He knew. I was simply the vessel that was being used.

Another visitor of the hotel walked in looking for his morning coffee. We began to speak about life, God, and so many other things. After much conversation, the three of us touched hands and prayed as a group. As the gentleman left, he looked at me and said, "Sister, I needed that."

After providing the church web site, showing her where to find the messages and encouraging her to keep the Word of God in her ear, it was time for me to leave. She came from behind the counter and gave me a strong hug. Before I left I said to her, "Get back to God, trust Him even when you can't trace Him."

I went to another hotel and asked to use the bathroom facilities and did my morning routine. As I turned, I looked myself in the mirror and silently asked, "Why are you here?

It was a simple question but it was much too deep this early in the morning. I finished up and headed out. At the local store, I bought a Styrofoam cooler, a plastic storage bin, a bag of ice, milk, water, juice, cheese, bread, mayo, some can goods, tuna, crackers, fruits and two cans of soda. I drove to the other side of the parking lot and began to adjust the trunk. The Styrofoam cooler would now become my "refrigerator"; the plastic storage bin would now become my dry "food pantry".

It was time to head to the other side of town. This would be my first Sunday away from church. I really did not like to miss church because it meant that I would be missing out on our church culture which included setting up for the worship experience, food being served, hugs, greetings, laughter, share your heart, a great praise and worship experience, a powerful impartation from the Pastor and many other things.

I began to reason with myself saying, "Well it's a season that I am in and like all seasons, it will come to an end. But, what is about to come to an end? Honestly, I am not in the mood to finish this thought this early on a Sunday morning." The drive was quiet and uneventful. I parked the car and waited in the parking lot of the local Barnes and Noble. Since I had about two hours left before going to work and was unable to attend the Sunday experience, I listened to the podcast of the Sunday message.

My smartphone now became a pulpit.

As I opened the trunk of the car, I had everything that was needed for this season of life. My wardrobe contained ten shirts, four pants, two pairs of comfortable work shoes, flip flops, necessary undergarments, sleepwear, active wear and something professional just in case. I had a Styrofoam fridge, a plastic food pantry, shopping bags with toiletries, a small red suit case with summer clothes, a black back pack with all important paperwork, a black trash bag for dirty clothes and a black trash bag with the blanket, pillow and sheet.

My life at forty-six was simple and easy; yet in disarray and in upheaval. It consisted of organized confusion. It made no sense yet made perfect sense. What a contradiction my life had become. I changed in the bathroom of the book store and then went out to organize the bits and pieces on the back seat of the car. It was time to pack away items that would not be used and prepare items that would be needed for bedtime. My t-shirt, night pant, head wrap, toothbrush, toothpaste, rag, soap and bottled water sat ready for use.

It was time for work. I closed the trunk and paused for a moment of reflection. Here is how I know that God is faithful to me. Right before I had to leave my apartment, I got up and went out with the mindset of determination. I said to myself, "I gotta find something that will bring in income." I sent out more than 67 applications and not one company responded, not one. Every door that I knocked on said, "No." Every person I reached out to said, "No." I sat in the house and simply said, "I am going to find a job locally and will not come home without one." I prayed and hit the bricks.

I went to several businesses in the neighborhood and they said, "No." Eventually, I was led to a local department store. I spoke with the general manager and was told they needed help in the ladies' department. I took the application home on a Tuesday, returned and interviewed on the following Wednesday, received the job offer on that Sunday and had to turn in my key for the apartment on Monday after.

The job paid enough to take care of car insurance, gas, groceries, laundry, and minor car repairs. I was able to save more than trinket money, but there was not enough to help me get an apartment or continue to pay my debtors on the prearranged payment plans.

My needs were being supplied and that was enough. Actually, it was more than enough. I truly appreciated the care from God, but I was concerned and confused about the self-care.

It was a good Sunday at work. There were a lot of after church shoppers, need something for Monday shoppers, getting ready to go on a long-awaited cruise shoppers, need some white linen for a party shoppers, and buying in bulk to send home to my country shoppers. Before I knew it, 7 o'clock had come and the day was over.

It's time to head home. I thought to myself, "What home we heading to Michele, when your actions ensured we don't have one?". Ouch! The truth cut me deep. Before heading to my next destination, I stopped at the local gas station to replenish the ice. What do I want to eat tonight? Tuna fish and crackers? Beans and tuna fish? Hot tea and crackers? Oatmeal? A cheese sandwich with mayo and mustard? A cup of soup noodles? The choices in my pantry were simple and so was my meal.

As I sat in the car, I felt at peace. But at peace with what exactly? What did I just accept? What is this current situation about to do for and in my life? It's definitely about to do something different in me. I know it. I feel it. I sense it. But I can't see it. Oh well, enough pondering for now. After my Sunday meal, I headed over to the old neighborhood.

I parked a few houses down from the house where my mom used to live and made my way to the back seat. The pillow, blanket and sheet were prepared and laid out on the back seat. The windows were cracked and there was a mixture of light and shade. I thanked God for His kindness and I slept.

I was not as fitful as the previous night but there was still a CODE RED in effect.

MY DAD'S BIBLE

Monday July 18th

It's 5:01am and I needed to talk.

"God, here is what is on my heart today." I told Him all of my concerns and fears. I thanked Him for grace and mercy, for a place to lay my head and for His kindness towards me. I asked for forgiveness for my sins, and I acknowledged that my disobedience played a part in why I am in this predicament. I asked for insight as to what else is wrong with me and admitted that embarrassment is why I won't tell my family about my present state of homelessness. I felt that my family had done more than enough already. I felt as if this life event called for my total surrender. It called for me to trust God more. This was between Him and me.

The Bible mentions taking no thoughts for tomorrow. I felt the need to read that. I knew it was in there somewhere. I had to find it. I reached for the Bible. It was my father's. The cover was spotted from wear and tear. The pages were worn. The book within was separated from the cover at the seams. There were pages that were falling out. It has been battle tested. It was very precious to me. Could I find it from memory? I thought to myself, "Let me see- let me see- let me see. No, not there. Not there. Wait! No, not there. Okay, there it is! The Sermon on the Mount, Matthew 6."

This was my first meal of the day and as I read, I began to get an understanding. Wait, did Jesus just speak to me? Did this Bible just speak to me 2000 years later and bring calm to my heart and comfort to my soul? Did I just get served another plate of "peace of mind?" Am I really not to worry about anything beyond today? Will you really work this out day by day? Will you truly provide for me daily? Then I heard a still, small voice and it simply said, "Look for me in the kindness of the people I have assigned to you daily."

Man, after reading that scripture, I exhaled. It felt like my mind walked up to God, crawled into His hands, and lied down to get some long overdue rest. I needed this scripture this morning. I have read it so many times but never related to it as I do now. At that moment, in this situation, that scripture had received new importance and significance in my life. The scripture became more than black words on white pages with red coloring for emphasis. It became the air I needed to breathe so that I could get through this season of my life, specifically today.

I was led to a popular Travel Inn. I took my items and walked in like I had just come from my room. I used the bathroom and took care of morning responsibilities. On my way out the waffles called my name and it was important to answer.

"Excuse me, do you mind if I help myself to breakfast?", I asked the attendant.

"Of course, you can," she responded.

Hot tea, apple juice, waffles, and morning news were on the menu. I marinated for as long as I could and savored each bite. On the way out, I thanked the front desk clerk for extending kindness towards me. I headed to the gas station. My routine consisted of emptying the melted ice that remained in the Styrofoam cooler, adjusting the items contained therein and using two overly large cups to fill the cooler with ice. I would then head to the local gym parking lot and park. I used this time to adjust the seats, clean the car, put away dirty items, get clothes ready for work, walk and stretch and then take a personal development phone call.

After about 80 minutes I went to the bookstore. Unfortunately, I could not stay longer because there was a nine-hour workday ahead of me. I retrieved my work clothes from the car, changed in the bookstore restroom and arrived at work at 11:00 am. It was long and hard. My back ached, my feet complained, and my arms were tired from carrying items. Interacting with the customers was the best part of the day.

It always was.

It's time to leave. I said good night to my coworkers and head to the car. I opened all four of my doors and felt the sticky heat escape. The leather seats were my worst enemy. Heat and humidity have formed a bond and decided to dwell in my car. Damn this heat! Damn you indeed! While the car cooled down I opened the trunk to get my change of clothes, toothbrush, toothpaste, 3 bottled waters, soap, washrag, undergarment, and daytime clothes for tomorrow.

Preparation precedes blessings. "This is only but a moment Michele; it will not be like this always. It's simply seasonal," I said to myself. That's a part of Self-Talk 101. Today's topic is on encouragement. Go THROUGH the process! GO through the process. GO THROUGH THE PROCESS!! I feel the need to listen to a sermon. I parked and secured the car, cracked the windows and adjusted the front seat.

The sermon gave me exactly what I needed. I caught a glimpse of myself in the rear-view mirror. "Go through Michele -do not die in the process- go through."

I believe I will hold on for another day.

TRUST GOD, EVEN WHEN YOU CAN'T TRACE GOD

Tuesday July 19th

Today I feel "some type of way".

Not up, not down, just "some type of way". I sat still. I was listening for something but what it was, I didn't know. When was the last time I dreamed? I'm not speaking of the type of dreaming that takes place when you are making achievements or plans, but a dream that occurs when I sleep. My intuition is very strong, even when I stifle it; it speaks very clearly. I felt a nudging. Almost as if a change is forth coming from this location. It's time to make an early move. I started the car and headed out. "Where am I going to start my day today, take the lead Lord," I said to myself. I was led right back to the Travel Inn on the other side of town.

I took my items and went inside and did the morning routine. Again, I asked if I could get breakfast. I enjoyed the same menu from the previous day. In the dining area the television was on. One thing I know about the morning news is that it is full of headlines that can start the day with a negative frame of mind. I could not linger too long today. After thanking the front desk clerk, I headed to the gas station and then to the gym parking lot to begin what was now becoming my routine.

As I drove past the book store, I saw a young lady that came out from her overnight hiding place behind a dumpster. I noticed she had 3 bags on her shoulders and was walking in the opposite direction. I pulled into the gym parking lot and parked. There are usually lots of early morning folks working out before the sun rise.

"Michele, do you realize just how blessed you are? Did you see the young lady who walked past you? You have a car to sleep in, 4 doors to lock, the ability to get from point A to point B without having to put all your items on your shoulder. You have a job. You still get a weekly check with your name on it. Granted, it's not enough to pay rent but it is enough to buy gas, food, pay car insurance and make minor repairs. You are in good health and you can still gather with the brethren on Wednesdays and pray, even if you cannot go to church on Sundays due to your work schedule. Michele, do you understand that it is the grace of God that prevents you from being in her shoes?" I said to myself.

I got out of the car and took a walk. Man, right there in the parking lot, I lifted my hands and prayed out loud and thanked God. "Lord, I thank you for this moment in my life. I know that poor decisions have placed me here. I know it's me. I truly believe that something good is coming out of this. I thank you for the job that you have provided. I thank you for the car that you are keeping together even though it needs major repairs, but day by day you cause it to remain faithful. I am grateful that your grace is keeping me from losing my mind. I am grateful that the angels you have given charge over me are keeping me by day and night. I am grateful for Your Word that feeds me and the sermons on the Victory Church Atl app that comforts me. I am grateful for health and strength, but more than anything, I am grateful that at the end of this season in my life, I will never be the same. What you want me to see and the lesson that you want me to understand, help me to finally get it. I love you and appreciate you very much God. This is my prayer to you, in Jesus' Name, Amen."

I went back to the car and leaned on the front hood and looked around. So many people were on their morning run, walk or stretch. Life was going on as usual. I wondered what "usual" would be for me after this life event.

I had an early day at work. I talked, smiled, helped and sold. Over all, I did really well.

After work, I headed to the gas station, replenished, refreshed, got needed items out of the trunk and made plans to head back to the same place. As I drove, I felt the need to hear a message on the

Victory Church Atl app. I listened to an old message titled: "Let It Die."

Man, when I tell you that I needed that, I am not kidding.

I had been reminiscing about an old love. I wondered how he was doing. I wondered if he was safe from harm. I wondered if he thought about me. What the what? Where did that thought come from? Oh well, at some point, I had to accept, that there would be no us. No more pining for him. Yes, the heart wants what it wants, but the head must weigh the pros and cons. He is a con, in so many ways.

"Just let it die Michele. Let It Die," I said to myself.

Wednesday July 20th

I thought to myself, "It's time to go somewhere different today to get started."

It was five o'clock in the morning and I could not go back to sleep.

I was in the driver's seat. I leaned it all the way back, tossed a sheet over myself, put the pillow behind my back and relaxed. I noticed that I was no longer on high alert. Does that mean that the "gorilla" has accepted that this is now where I am in my life until further notice?

I was about to get out of the car when I felt the need to wait. I began to settle into the seat a little more when I saw the light of a car. It cruised slowly through the neighborhood. It was a police car. I stayed low. It drove slowly as it passed by, made a turn at the end of the block and was creeping back up the block. I did not realize that I stopped breathing until it was out of sight.

I sat still and waited. When my nerves were settled, I came out the car and stretched. After looking around the neighborhood, it was time to get the day started. Right turn, left turn, right turn again, a left turn, and then another left turn. Okay, right here. Well, this will definitely do. This place is what I deeply needed this morning. I took my leisure in washing up and getting ready for the day. I headed to the local gas station to get ice for the fridge and hot water for the oatmeal. I arrived at the gym parking lot and saw the usual morning workout crowd. I came out of the car, stretched, walked then returned and made sure the inside was clean and presentable. I read my Bible, ate and enjoyed some personal development for about an hour and a half.

I attempted to go to the bookstore to read, but I had a sudden urge to leave. Hmmm? Ooookkkkay. I continued to drive: right, left, then another left. I parked under a shaded tree. I jumped out, popped the trunk and began to clean it out. A young man came along with his little brother. He walked passed me and sat in his car. His little brother was running in and out of and around the car. I walked over and introduced myself to him. He was twenty two and his brother was five. "Would you like something cold to drink?" I asked. "Yes" the little brother answered for both of them. We walked to my car and he looked inside the trunk. "You look prepared for anything". If only he knew. I opened the Styrofoam fridge and offered them some cold water. "Aaah" was what I heard his little brother say.

"Kindness is so important but, sometimes when it is extended to someone, they look for the string that is attached," I said to him.

"In this moment, with this hot ass Georgia sun, your kindness is doing a lot for me and my brother," he said.

He looked at me and then at his little brother. His little brother went off to play by the car. "How is life treating you young man?" I asked. "It's kicking my ass. At times I feel like "yeah, I got this" and know exactly what to do. At other times I feel like it has me by my nuts and got me on my knees". I noticed he kept looking at his little brother with an appreciative type of love. "You know my brother is a miracle. My mother was told she could not have more kids but she did not accept it. She tried and boom there he is. I wish me and my moms could agree but we don't see eye to eye no more. I haven't always made smart decisions and she reminds me of it. She wants me to do what she wants me to do, but I got dreams she can't see".

His eyes were firmly planted on watching out for his little brother but his mind was somewhere else. "You guys look hungry. I would like to share some snacks with you" I said. He called his little brother over and we began to eat in silence. "Why you got so much stuff in your trunk?" He asked me. "Life events have occurred and I am adjusting to it. It ain't easy, but I believe that I will be better because of it. I just gotta trust God. I might not have nuts, but these events got me on my knees praying like never before" I said. He laughed out loud at what I said. "You know what Michele since I'm on my knees, I guess I will also pray like never before too".

I asked if I could pray with him and he said yes. The little brother joined us and held my hand. We prayed. I believe he got what he needed. He hugged me and said, "Thank you."

"Make wiser decisions," I said but then I heard my gorilla say, "Yeah right, Michele, you are not one to even try to talk right now. Remember the situation we are in, right?" I immediately fell quiet.

"Wisdom comes from reading Proverbs," he said. I agreed 100%. As his mother came out from the store, we hugged and said our goodbyes. I stayed under that tree confused, stumped and amazed. The thing I truly didn't understand and the question I asked myself is why would God use me at what I felt was the most unqualified, awkward and confused time of my life. Why use me to tell someone about His goodness and His love? Does He not see that I don't have it together and I am a hot mess?

I had the day off so I stayed in the neighborhood. My mechanic inspected the car the previous month and told me, in the simplest way, "The car is riding on faith. There are many repairs that are needed. I strongly advise you to stay local because you might not make it back if you go far." I was driving the car under a warranty called Grace.

During the day, I received three phone calls from some of my Kingdom sisters. They each ended the conversation in prayer. To me, their prayers were the oxygen that my soul needed. Every single one of them prayed exactly what I needed to get me through that day.

I was refreshed and replenished.

It was time for Access. It's when the brethren from Victory Church Atl gather, once a week, and have one hour of prayers. I looked forward to being there. I walked in, found a corner, and got on my knees. I could not pray. I was so full. All I could do was cry because my heart was overwhelmed with gratitude. "Thank you, God, for this season of my life," I said as my tears became my prayers.

Afterwards, I said my goodbyes and made my way to the gas station to get some needed items. I wondered where I would be parking to sleep tonight. I sat still and waited to be led. As I started the car and began to drive, I turned on the Victory Church Atl app and listened to a message from the "Be Set Free" message series call "Stripped for Greater".

I now understood where I was in my adult life. I was being stripped for greater. The season of my life had been identified and named; I could endure what I was going through.

Understanding is very important to me and now that my life event was identified, it gave me insight like I never had before. This moment of lack had its own abundance and overflow. There was wealth in the intangibles and that was what I was receiving. This was a time of letting go. There was a specific thing that was about to leave my life forever. This stripping was a needed requirement.

It was preparation. Whatever was about to be stripped MUST go or else it would be a hindrance in my next season.

The message rocked me to sleep.

Thursday July 21st

I remember waking up thanking God for another day of hope after a night of safety.

My mind began jumping to many different topics. I needed my mind to settle down because it was way too soon for chaos and organized confusion at 5 o'clock in the morning. I drove to the new location to take care of morning responsibilities and then it was off to the gas station for ice, hot water, and a snack.

I decided to stay put for a couple of moments because I didn't feel like being in the morning traffic. As I meditated, my mind began to reminisce about the encounter I had with the owner of a local laundromat. We spoke about so many different topics. We talked about his home life, his mother who prays two hours each day, and his daughter who is about to go to college. We talked about his life as an engineer, a traveler, and his interest in visiting the largest church in Korea. We discussed the real reason why a foreign-made car is a good investment and the importance of being a valuable asset. We also discussed why one should arrive ten minutes early to work and leave ten minutes later. He told me why he does not fight with his wife and why God is good all the time.

He truly was a kind man.

I started the car and continued my morning in the gym parking lot. I stretched, walked, inhaled deeply, exhaled and bathed my face with the morning sun. I read Proverbs. I read what the fool does and what he gets and what the wise does and gets. Whelp, there I was all up in the Bible- damn fool!

I did my personal development, cleaned the car, packed a lunch from my cooler and headed to the local book store. I read some magazines about travel and then read *"Awaken the Giant Within"* by Tony Robbins. The book was reading me and helped bring new understanding.

Rain began to lightly fall. I love the rain! I grabbed my belongings, ran to the car, stretched out in the driver's seat and slept as the rain fell. When I awoke, I read the first three chapters of Esther until I dozed off again. I awoke looking up at the moon-roof in the car.

It was late in the afternoon. Time to head to the gas station. The night before, I saw a lady sitting in her car with lots of clothing and home goods piled into her back and front seat. Like me, she was parked there for a while. I went to her car and asked her if it would be alright to buy her a meal or something cold. She refused.

I returned to the car, turned on the church app on my phone and listened to another message series I enjoy called Abba. The topic was "Prototype."

When I arrived at my location, I was about to park but then I felt a strong notion to park elsewhere. I could not sleep. I changed sleeping positions many times but could not find the right position. It was after midnight and I was wide awake. The sleep from earlier was a good deep sleep. The rain helped me to unwind. So here I am at 12:15 in the morning, bright-eyed and bushy-tailed.

Biblegateway.com is my favorite website to listen to the audio Bible. I was in the mood to listen to the rest of Esther. I found it comforting. I was at a loss for words when I listened to the courage that Esther showed as she went in faith to meet the King knowing that she could be killed.

Perhaps one day I will have that magnitude of courage.

INTIMACY

IN. TO. ME . I.

DESIRE. FOR.

YOU. TO. SEE

Friday July 22nd

Friday...it was Friday.

You know, there was a time in my life when I would celebrate Fridays. It indicated that the work week, referred to at my job as "Day five of the hostage situation," had come to an end and I made it through. However, I worked retail and retail makes the majority of their money Friday through Sunday. I was expecting something from God that day and it was something to be done that only He could do.

I had an okay night. I found myself questioning why I was in a position of sacrifice and lack. I wondered if there was a place inside of me that feeds pain and guilt. Did I secretly need to be in agony and love feeling pain? What is it exactly? Do I need to feel that I have earned the right to have something good and suffering was the way to prove it? There was a splinter that was lodged in my psyche that needed to be identified and removed, but it could only be done with understanding. At this point, I needed to be honest with myself and say, "I don't understand."

I was sabotaging myself. I knew it and I felt it. I was on a psychological hamster wheel and I needed it to stop. But the "how" kept evading me because the "why" had not been answered.

I was tired and getting older. At 46, I thought I would have had it all together, but I found myself constantly starting over. I had enough of this……thing……this…..splinter……this……whatever the hell it was.

The loudest sound in the world is silence and I sat in it for a good hour. I could not look at myself in the mirror and I had a hard time facing myself that day. I did not want to look "me" in the eyes. I was simply too disappointed.

I did my morning routine and went to the gym parking lot. I stretched, walked and then headed to the car to read the Bible. After I read, I put it down and prepared myself for some tough thoughts. I got out of the car and went walking again. "Where am I emotionally? Where am I spiritually? Where am I financially? Where am I in my thinking? Where am I in my faith? Where am I in trusting God? Where am I in my belief?" I asked myself.

It was time for some truth. It was the type of truth that needed to be said out loud. Would I offend God if I told Him what I was wrestling with? Would it insult Him after all He had done for me? Would it bring shame to me if I admitted out loud what I was struggling with internally? Would He separate Himself from me? After all He has done, I should have a different perspective, right? I believe the time has come to tell Him out loud what I already knew internally. Look, let's cut the bullshit. He Is God, and since He *is* God, there is no such thing as breaking news to Him. The fact is, He already knows, and He is waiting on me to be honest with MYSELF. He is waiting for me to admit it out loud, so *my* ears can hear it. But when I do, what happens next? Well I guess that is what I would find out because I was not going to hold it in and pretend any longer.

Well, I opened my mouth and said, "God, I believe but help the part of me that has un-belief. I don't trust you anymore and my faith is wavering. I am frustrated belonging to you. You are silent when I need you to speak. You are elusive when I need you to be near. Belonging to you always requires sacrifice but I am tired of sacrificing for your name's sake. I am sick of being yours. I can't stand it anymore! I want to walk away but then where am I going to go? Will I go to the enemy? Don't I have a say in what I choose for me? I have been raised in the church but church ain't working for me anymore. Something is shifting in me that require more. I am sick of this shit. I just don't... I can't...it's just...you know what... I've had enough. Yeah, I know what you have done for me since I have been homeless, and I know how you have covered me and taken care of me all my life, but I want more.

This agitation in me is causing me to be angry and pissed off and...I can't continue like this...I just can't with you...I just can't."

I stopped walking. "Did I just say out loud what was really in my heart towards God? What the fuck was I thinking?" I said.

My mind was silent. My heart was beating loudly in my chest. I could still hear, see, taste, smell and touch. I could still walk and think. There was no crack in the sky where thunder was rolling and lightening was about to strike. There was no hail that was sent to strike me on the head. The earth did not split wide open and devour me and half of the neighborhood. There was not an appearance of my name on a tombstone showing: born 1969, died 2016, reason: "She told God what was truly in her heart towards Him."

There were people doing their morning routines as well as the comings and goings of cars. I exhaled loudly. I sat in the car, waiting. I don't know what I was waiting for, but I was waiting.

An older couple drove up to my car. They were looking for a store in the area. I called the store, got the directions, and said, "Follow me." We drove for about seven minutes. I led them straight to the place. I was about to drive away when the elderly gentleman asked me to wait. He got out of the truck, gave me a hug and $5 and said, "God Bless You." I did not know what to say. All I knew was that the conversation I had with God earlier was emotionally draining, honest and scary for me. I nodded my head, got in the car and drove away.

At the local book store, I sat and wrote. I searched my social media for updates, spoke with folks on the phone, and enjoyed a sandwich. It was time for work. I got changed and headed to take care of responsibilities that had my name attached to them. It was a good Friday. It was busy enough to make the time pass quickly yet slow enough that you could catch your breath. After work, I got ready for the night. I drove to my typical spot in the neighborhood. My sleep was fitful. I was up, tossing and turning. I just could not sleep. I was looking around. I had to pray and ask for help.

"Wait a minute, didn't you tell God about your emotional and mental state towards Him earlier and now you are feeling "some type of way" so you want to pray? That is some hypocritical, schizophrenic, use God conveniently when it benefits you behavior. You know that, right? You know that you are taking God's grace for granted, right? You know you are wrong, right?" I said to myself.

My conscious was truthful. I could not argue against that fact.

I started the car, put it in reverse and found another spot that felt safer. As I turned off the engine, there was a thought that found its way to me. "I wonder, was I wrong for telling God the truth that was in my heart and soul? Did I go too far? Was I wrong for being transparent about my frustrations and anger?"

I turned on the audio Bible.

My tenseness began to dissipate.

I laid back and slept.

Saturday July 23rd

It was early morning. The earth is old and new.

I thanked all the hosts of heaven for their commitment to my care. I thanked God for His compassion and understanding. I never understood the contradiction that was involved in this relationship between God and mankind. I have longed to have a better understanding of this relationship that exists between God and me. I wanted to draw closer to Him, but I needed to know that I still had a choice to be away from Him at the same time and be alright.

I wanted to know that I would still be myself and belong to Him. I wanted to change but remain the same. It's both selfish and conditional.

There are many definitions of the word relationship. One meaning is: *the way in which two or more concepts, objects, or people are connected, or the state of being connected.* When I was younger, I was told, "Never question God. You don't have the right to question God." There was a time in my life when I accepted that but not anymore. I have been through too much in my life. Why should I be afraid to ask and entertain the question, "Why God?" If I am in a relationship with God, I am not supposed to be afraid of Him. Why would I want to be in a relationship and be afraid? Why would I want to be in a relationship and not be able to speak my mind? Am I in a relationship or is this a dictatorship?

Why would I want to be in a relationship and talk to everyone else about my feelings but not go to the one that is a part of my source of frustration and agitation? What exactly did I want from God? What questions was I supposed to ask but was afraid to ask because I just might get the answer? Why was I changing and no longer satisfied with myself and how I was with Him? Why was I blaming Him? Why God? Why?

The foundation on which I was built, was no longer working. I had outgrown a lot of biblical teachings and what I once accepted without question, I was now questioning. Church lingo was not satisfying me anymore. I have outgrown it. Sunday school teachings are no longer answering questions. Life experiences and events have shattered me to the point where my mind, body, soul and spirit were looking for more. More of what, from where and from whom?

Another definition of the word relationship is: *a state of affairs existing between those having relations or dealings; a romantic or passionate attachment.* BAM! That was it. That was the understanding that I was looking for and the missing ingredient in our relationship. That was the source of my frustration. I did not have a passionate attachment to God. I was not in love with God. I was not in love with the one I was in a relationship with. I was not intimate with Him. I became comfortable with Him. I expected from Him. I demanded from Him. I argued with Him. I fussed Him out and blamed Him.

When He corrected my behavior, I became like a spoiled child, stomping off and being disobedient to teach Him a lesson. I wanted to hurt Him for loving and taking good care of me. I was selfish in the relationship. I was rude in the relationship. I was callous in the relationship. "When I need you, God, I will let you know but when I don't need You, please leave me alone. Why do I gotta do for you God? Ain't it all about me?" This is what I would say to Him.

I mean really, since I'm being honest, why would anyone want to be in a relationship with such a selfish bitch like me? I wanted God to make me fall in love with Him in a way that worked for me. However, if He must put on a performance and constantly prove Himself, I would be putting Him in a posture of being manipulated by my emotions, mental state and whims. That's real talk. Didn't He already provide everything that this relationship and my life required?

Didn't He give everything this relationship and my life would need for us to be a success with each other? So, the problem was not Him. The problem was me.

I went to my usual spot, but because it was the weekend, there were a lot of people in and out. I tried to look for another location but when I went into their bathroom, I felt uncomfortable. I drove back to the first spot. "Lord, all I need is seven minutes, seven. If you could give me seven minutes of uninterrupted time, it would be much appreciated," I said.

I began to take care of my morning duties. I was like a person on Black Friday going after the last 60-inch flat screen TV for $100. I moved with speed and haste. All was put together and in place in eight minutes.

For me, that was a personal best. I drove out and headed to get my ice and hot water. I had to be at work early that morning. I greeted the customers, laughed, and brushed off the attitude of those who were negative. The manager had a nasty attitude towards me when I left my area and escorted a customer to another area of the store. He attempted to get smart with me. I simply brushed the dirt off my shoulders and kept moving. He sheepishly approached me with an apology mixed with a reason to justify his behavior. Again, I brushed the dirt off my shoulder.

I left early and had time to enjoy the evening. The local bookstore was where I ended up. Travel magazines and biographies were calling my name. I received a phone call from my friend Robert. He called to make sure I was okay. We spoke for about an hour and ended in prayer. He will be a great husband and father one day.

I headed outside and lingered by the car for some reason. There was a driver that asked if I was the one who called for him. I told him no. He explained to me that this was his first time with Uber. He shared his concerns about this choice of work. I asked him if it would be alright if we prayed. He agreed. After the prayers, he looked at me and said, "You truly are a blessing. Tonight, you are a sent angel."

"You know what, I receive that. God be glorified," I replied.

I went inside my car and headed to the local gas station. I got everything I needed and turned on the audio Bible. I was in the mood to listen to the book of Matthew. "I want intimacy with you God. Intimacy. I want to know what falling in love with You is really like. I want to love You with my heart and soul and spirit. I want to see You. The only question I have is what will it cost me?" I asked.

I arrived at the secured place, parked, and thanked Jesus for His presence, and that was that.

Sunday July 24th

It was Sunday. I was fatigued.

My mind hurts. My body hurts. I was operating on five hours of sleep. I woke up in a car that was holding on by grace. My feet hurt and I had to go to work. I greeted God, Jesus, the Holy Spirit and the Angels that God had given charge over me. I did not feel like writing much. I didn't feel like much of anything really.

I started to slip into familiarity and routine in a situation that was not normal for me.

It was a long day. I was disturbed all day. I got into a verbal altercation with my manager. Man, let me tell you, the part of me that wanted to dismantle her was on the edge of being released! Thankfully, I refused to let that gorilla out. The day was long and hot.

When the day was over, the car was hot and sticky.

Leather in the summertime is not cute. I needed a shower, a real one! The type of shower where you stand under the water and let it run all over your parts. Where it starts out hot but you stay so long the water begins to gradually get cold.

I longed for a soft bed.

My mind replays the conflict. Today sucked and I couldn't sleep.

Monday July 25th

I have an unusual ache in my body this morning.

Was it from the position in which I slept? Was it because of stress from my current situation? Was it simply old age introducing itself to me? I didn't know how much more of this I could take. It was time to decide. I woke up at 3:34a.m. and could not go back to sleep. I was having conversations with myself about where I was, why I was here, what happened, and how come. It was time to leave. I knew it. Why was I still lingering? Why?

It was time to go!

I thanked the heavenly host for a safe night sleep. Took time to do a deep stretch this morning. My body thanked me for it. It was time to get the morning routine started. I ate an early breakfast and made my way to work. My mind and body was tired. I was functioning on auto pilot. My customers gave me a day full of, "Remove this," "Add this," "Find this," or "Does this come in a size 11?"

My coworker asked, "Ms. Michele, you okay? You have not smiled all day."

I truly valued him saying that. I did not know that he was paying attention. He gave me a hug and encouraged me. I needed that kind gesture. I thanked him and continued the day. As I was walking away, I remembered why I stayed away from retail work. It is not for everyone. I really believe you must be called, set aside and hand-crafted by God Himself to work in retail. In that moment, I decided I was leaving that job. I thought, "When I get my paycheck, I am cashing it, buying a plane ticket and leaving. I am waiting no longer."

After work ended I went to the bookstore and stayed in the parking lot. I went to the trunk to get an item, and then closed it. As soon as it slammed I remembered I needed something else. When I tried to open it, the trunk refused to open. I used the button from inside the car and it refused to open. I tried the key and it still refused to open. I pulled, pushed, prodded, prayed, and cussed and still, no luck.

Damnnnn! Noooooo! Shitttttttttt! All of the supplies and items needed were locked in that trunk. Everything was in that trunk.

"Can anything—"

"HOLD IT RIGHT THERE MICHELE!"

I knew I was about to get checked.

"Before you let anything else come out of your mouth, think about what you are about to say."

I knew it was the Holy Spirit. I had to be mindful of my tongue. I froze mid-sentence.

"Remember Michele, death and life is in the power of the tongue."

I kept silent. Then I began to laugh.

It was an uncontrollable, loud, what the hell, I ain't gonna let this get to me, the Holy Spirit just checked me, this too shall pass, what a day laugh. From my toe, from my soul, I ain't gonna lose my mind, I'm gonna make it through this, kind of laugh.

"Well Michele, what we gonna do now?" I did what I know how to do. I began to praise God and said, "Thank You Jesus!" Then a song came to my mind and I sang, "You're a good, good, Father, it's who You are, it's who You are, it's who You are, and I'm loved by You, it's what I am, it's what I am, it's what I am." Man, listen, my spirit lifted.

"Satan, let me talk to you. You won't win. I may have my issues with God, but I respect Him. You just gonna have to beat it, you are already defeated!"

The laughter started to come up from my soul again and exploded. It was an uncontrollable fit of laughter. Joy found its way into the middle of my pain. Wow, that was awesome. After I regained my senses I simply said, "Well God, what's next?"

I started the car and headed to Walmart.

I bought these emergency items: water, toothpaste, toothbrush, rags, soap, undergarments, tee-shirt and other items. I drove to an empty spot in the Walmart parking lot, refreshed myself, changed and asked God to lead me where I was supposed to sleep that night.

I slept in the driver's seat that night. I simply leaned the seat back, stretched out my legs, got my pillow and sheet, put on the audio Bible and exhaled.

I am in the mood to hear the Book of Joshua.

I fell into a deep sleep.

Tuesday July 26th

Man listen, I felt so refreshed.

I got five straight hours of sleep. My mind was settled and at peace. I got out of the car and checked the trunk. Still locked. Oh well, I figured I would have to go to the mechanic later that day. I thanked God for His Grace and Mercy. I noticed I had started to like God a lot more. Ever since I was transparent and got those words and that feeling out, I had been more accepting of the fact that telling Him how I felt was the best thing I could have done.

I also began to think that He liked me too.

One characteristic I had noticed that I really admired about God was that He was very patient with me. I mean, veerryyy patient. I also noticed that he extended a lot of Grace to me. I mean a loooottttt of Grace. Why would He want my company and my presence? Maybe He knows something about me that I don't know. Oh well, all I knew was that there was something different about me and how I felt about God this morning. I truly liked Him from my heart.

I inhaled until no more air could get into my lungs, and then exhaled until I almost passed out. What a rush.

It was time to get the day started. I went to the usual morning spot but it was not available. I drove to another location and it was just what I needed. I opened the back door and got out all the items that would be needed. I took the most refreshing shower one could from a water bottle at 6:42 a.m.

After everything was in place, I went to the back seat and looked at the middle arm rest. I lowered the arm rest and pulled open a plastic cover and there it was. I now had access to the trunk. I looked at the inside lock and simply focused on it. I got out of the car, put the key into the outside lock, turned the key with all the faith I had and then click, pop. The trunk opened.

YEAH!!! LOOK AT GOD!!!

To make sure it would continue to open and close, I used some olive oil, yes, olive oil (I keep some in my purse). I greased the lock and everything connected to it. I then open and closed that trunk until my hands were tired. When I was satisfied, I cleaned up the area, cleaned up the car, got out the items I would need for the day and put them on the back seat. I drove to get gas, hot water and ice for my fridge. In the parking lot, I ate a breakfast of tuna fish and crackers with hot tea. I got out my headphones and my Bible. I plugged my headphones into my telephone. Instead of music or the audio Bible, I felt this over whelming urge to pray.

I had an overwhelming desire to pray for all my old relationships, all the damage and hurt that I was still carrying for what they did to me and all the wrong I did to them. I got out of the car and started to pray and called each of them by name and prayed about each specific event. Man, those prayers came from a deep place. Some were more painful than others. Tears were finding its way down my face, but I did not care. Now was the assigned time to release and forgive.

There was one man that cut me the deepest and I had trouble letting go of the pain, but now was the time. I forgave him for many wrongs and released him from the part of my heart that despised him.

I asked God to forgive me for holding on to hatred and to bless each of them wherever they may be. There was still one I was not ready to forgive. I have a knife for his throat. I asked God to help me unwrap from the hatred. I will get to the place of forgiveness, but I was not there yet with him. No need for pretense, it is what it is.

"Goodbye to all the ghost of my past. I no longer desire to conjure you up in my thinking or replay the events. It is finished."

I washed my face and stood in the sun for a moment. I had the unction to read Job 42. I was stuck at verse 5. It stated the following, "My ears had heard of you but now my eyes have seen you." I noticed two key things that struck me. The first was in verse 10. Job prayed for his friends and then God accepted his prayers. After that, restoration came to Job. But there was an even greater revelation for me and it spoke to me from verse 5. "My ears had heard of you but now my eyes have seen you." Wait a minute, did I read that right?

Job is in a relationship with God, his faith is tested, he is going through hell, begins to complain and tells God what is on his heart.

The circumstances overwhelmed him so much so that he vents. After Job gets it off his chest, God has a response for Job and called Job on the carpet.

However, it was not until God put Job in check and told Job, "Man up, I'm going to question you, Job, and you are going to answer me" and asked Job to give an account of his whereabouts when the foundation of the world was being laid that something happens.

Are you telling me that after it was all said and done, the greatest gift that Job received was not all the tangibles that were recovered, but the fact that he could now "see" God? Why is it he could not "see" God before? How blind was his mind? Is my mind blind also? Are you telling me that Job received his sight (insight or understand) because he went through hell? Did he receive a deeper revelation of who God was because of what he had been through? Is that what I just read? Because if that's what I just read, then the blessing was not the "things" Job received at the latter end of his life, but seeing God was the blessing.

 It was the purpose for the test.

Is that what I just saw? Is that what I just read? Why do I feel like in this season, a part of me can identify with Job? Am I Job? Am I going to see God like never before? I had to ponder those questions, but I was uncomfortable going there in my thoughts.

I felt clean, from the inside. I felt like a stumbling block had been removed. I feel ready. From deep within, I knew it. I was in preparation mode for something. Was it for a relationship? Was it a deeper understanding of God? Would I also "see" God like Job did? If so, how would God present himself to me? What would He look like?

I was stuck in pondering mode.

It was after 9:00am. I was late for my personal development call. I joined in, sent some text messages to check in with the people who were on my heart, wrote some, and then went to the bookstore and decompressed. I called my friend Joseph to check in. He was on my mind and I wanted to make sure he was well. I have learned that when someone is on my mind, call them. This could be the day that he needed to know a friend cares. He answered and he began to share his heart with me. He was going through. Because it was almost time for me to head to work, I asked if we could speak after work.

Overall the day at work was good, I think. I really was not there. After work I headed to the gas station and got everything I needed. Joseph called back and we spoke for over an hour. His heart was full and his situation was just as rough as mine.

I am so grateful that we reconnected. Our conversations were edifying, confronting, truthful, correcting, encouraging and funny. We always ended in a prayer.

I love and value him from a place called "gratefulness and appreciation."

It was time to leave where I was. I drove to the safe spot. After parking I looked around. The neighborhood was truly quiet. I put the blanket behind my back for support, put the pillow under my neck and covered with the sheet. The front seat would be my hammock yet another night.

The gospel of St. John rocked me to sleep. The atmosphere inside the car was charged with hope.

The atmosphere inside my mind was charged with hope. I felt safe from harm.

I slept soundly.

THE ENEMY OF FAITH IS NOT DOUBT, IT'S CERTAINTY

INTERMISSION

Now listen to me.

Are you listening? I'm going to tell you something that most Christians won't tell you and I hope you can handle this transparency.

The reality of the situation is, there *is* a psychological agony and an emotional upheaval and pain that is connected to walking by faith. It will stretch you and cost you.

It is life breaking and life altering.

We quote it, sing it, shout it, but how many of us can really relate to a life that walks by faith? Are you prepared to accept the process that comes with being stripped for greater?

Our experiences might be different but the blueprint has been laid.

Are you prepared to lose it? What if the price is everything?

I heard my pastor, Philip Anthony Mitchell, say something that have engraved itself into me and it was the following, "The enemy of or the opposite of faith is not doubt... it's certainty."

He also said "you must learn to trust God even when you can't trace God".

When you begin to walk by faith, you may find yourself saying the following statement many times, "God help me because I honestly don't know what to do, what to say, what to think, how to be." Sometimes the only prayer that can be said is, "God have mercy."

I wanted to tell God how to process my "next." I wanted to tell God what should be done, what content should be used, how it would work, and what was comfortable for me, because this isn't it.

I'm sure He probably shook His head and said, "Michele, you said you wanted to know Me intimately. You want to trust Me. You want me to reveal Myself to you and give you more of Me and less of you. Now you want to dictate the HOW. Really Michele? Really?".

My faith walk is traumatizing.

Yours may be different.

Here is what I know for sure. Jesus will NEVER leave you or forsake you. His is not a character of abandonment.

Wednesday July 27th

It was early in the morning and my mind was at ease.

Old thoughts tried to sneak in, but you know what, I'm done. I had a good night's sleep, really good! I think I was learning to rest in God. I stopped trying to be my own keeper. I remember my grandmother used to say, "God does not slumber, and He does not sleep, so why are you still up?" I am so glad He does not.

After clean-up duties, I headed to the gas station for ice and hot water. I was filling my fridge with ice when a gentleman said to me, "I would like to buy you a bag of ice." I said, "Thank you for your kindness, perhaps next time." My cooler was one cup of ice away from being full. In the gym parking lot, I stretched, walked and read the Bible.

For some reason, I kept going back to Job 42 verse 5. I kept seeing that Job saw God. I kept seeing that he clearly stated, "My ears had heard of you but now my eyes have seen you" (KJV). Does that mean that all this time Job was in a relationship with God but did not experience Him intimately until the crisis occurred?

I could not stop thinking about that question.

It was my day off and I chose not to be all over the place. I could not take a chance with the car. I headed to the dollar store to get some items. As I was leaving I was standing at the register and felt this pull towards the cashier. I felt like I was supposed to speak to him about something, but I hesitated. I thanked him and was about to walk out but the pull was stronger than before. I went up to him and looked him straight in his eyes.

"Young man, listen to me. You got to listen and do what God is telling you. You gotta make the decision to obey God and let things happen."

"Why are you telling me this?" he said to me. His eyes were fighting to hold back the tears that were ready to make their own decision to fall.

"Because there are lives that are attached to you making the decision." I said to him.

"Who told you to tell me this?" he said.

"God. It's time son." I left and did not look back.

I spent the day at the local book store. My mind loves to learn.

I read, wrote, looked at social media, read some more, sat in the car, text people who were in my heart, ate and strolled. I headed to Access to pray. Joining my brethren in prayer made my soul sing. I got what was needed for the night then headed to the assigned place to sleep.

I opened my Bible and put it on the dashboard of the car. I will read it tomorrow.

I leaned back and slept.

MY ROAD DOG: BUSTER THE PLANT

Thursday July 28th

Why am I still here in Atlanta?

It's time to leave. I feel as if I am taking advantage of God's grace and mercy by being here. It's time to go. There is a signal that is causing me to not become antsy but has me alert. A sensitivity of time and a window that is open and is on tick-tock count down mode. It's time to go.

I thanked God for today. Went to take care of my morning duties and decided to wash my hair. How in the world am I supposed to do that? Oh well. With 2 bottles of water I got started. Half of the first bottled saturated the hair. Then I put on shampoo and conditioner at the same time. I got a good lather and scrubbed the scalp and hair, roots to end. I then used the rest of the first bottle and the entire second bottle to rinse. I took a towel and dried my hair and then put a Walmart plastic bag over it to keep moist. My hair is very thick and if I leave it be, it will matte.

I got my comb, grease, hair moisture for twisting and put all of it on the front seat. I put away all the unneeded items in the trunk and off I went for ice and hot water. Then it was off to the parking lot of the gym. I spent time stretching; reading the bible, personal development, decompressing and then it was time to tackle my hair.

When it was over, I headed to the local bookstore. Today would be an easy day.

I went to the car to get an item but decided to stay a while. I wanted to listen to Colossians. As I put it on, I reached for my bible. I open it last night and did not read it. As I reached for it, I saw it was open to Colossians. I smiled. "See God, this is why I like you. It's the little things you do," I said to myself then I listened and read.

On the days I have off, I rest. I stay off my feet as much as possible and read.

Today I slept. Why would I want to sleep in a car with leather seats in this heat of over 90 degrees? It's because my body demanded it.

After a good couple of hours sleep I headed back to the book store. The time passed slowly today.

Eventually evening fell and the bookstore would be closing soon.

I headed to take care of nighttime routine and drove to the spot. I felt as if I needed to sleep and be easy. There is something that is soon coming that would require more of me.

I fell asleep as soon as my head hit the pillow.

Friday July 29th

It's beginning to get dangerous at the usual early morning spot.

I felt a sense of "urgency" in my spirit when I arrived closed to 6:30pm. I did a waterfall shower. As soon as I dried and put my clothes on, there was another driver that pulled up.

After all of the usual morning hub-bub, I went to the bookstore to read, write and think. What am I going to do next? What am I purposed to do next? I cannot see it.

It was time for work and I was glad. When I got there, one of my co-workers began to inform me of what I needed to do to stay ahead of the game. She warned me about who and what to watch out for. It was the right intention, but something about what she said did not feel right. There was a personal pain that was not being spoken about but was being projected.

I recognized her frustration. I received a check in my spirit. It felt like a warning telling me to beware of the one who is actually speaking. I was reminded not to let the outside environment and the negative folks inside. Don't let the water come in and flood the boat. I am passing through only. I was reminded not to get pulled in.

I purposed to have a great day at work and I did. I made lots of sales and met some great folks today.

I left work in high spirits.

Lately, I felt that I have slipped on my time with God. I have been listening to the Book of James, John, Hebrews and Deuteronomy a lot but not having heart to heart talks with Him. The words in the bible comfort me, but intimate time with God rescues me and eases my mind.

It's late.

Saturday July 30th

Good morning. I am still alive.

God is so good. Despite this current situation, what is missing and what is lacking, I have so much to appreciate Him for.

I am getting antsy sleeping in this neighborhood. Something is changing. I feel that I am being watched. Maybe it's me being hyper sensitive. Maybe it's not me and my intuition is correct. I am looking up at the roof of the car.

There is pain in my body today. It has been increasing a lot since this season of my life. I think I need to do a deep yoga stretch today. As I drove away from the neighborhood, I looked at it like a suspect. The biggest mistake to make is to stay in a place longer that what is necessary.

I was on the lookout for a new place to get my morning routine done. I had absolutely no idea where I was going but I have faith that I would be led to it. I went into the local Shell Station, looked around and decided it would work. After my morning responsibilities, it was time for the gym parking lot. I did yoga and additional stretching today.

I needed a treat so it was time for a waffle, but when I walked into the waffle place, my appetite changed to hash browns instead. Perhaps I needed some calcium also. I was not in the mood to remain indoors. I got my food as takeout and headed back to the gym parking lot. I enjoyed the hash browns and greedily devoured 2 cups of milk. It was also time to feed my spirit, so I listened to Deuteronomy 4. I really like the Old Testament.

I cleaned the car while my food digested and then headed to the bookstore.

Today I was drawn to read a book by TD Jakes Titled *Instincts*. A lot of what I read fell into my garden.

I went to work today and was surprised by a customer. I helped her make some decisions the previous weekend and she surprised me with some items as a gesture to say, "thank you." It was appreciated.

This was a tax-free weekend and the store was jam-packed with folks buying stuff just because. We had some great sales and I really enjoyed the customers. Another lady shared her heart with me and we prayed once we finished conversing.

I was kept busy that day. When the workday was over, my coworkers and I were too exhausted to do much of anything except to say, "see you tomorrow."

Listen, my feet were burning and very angry with me. That night I had spinach, carrots, brown rice, herring and cheese with a cup of tea for dinner.

It was lovely.

I was driving around deciding where to park and sleep for the night when I had the strangest intuition to go back to the neighborhood but park in a different spot. I waited until after 11:30pm and drove through with my headlights off. I parked in a different spot and settled down in the front seat.

Tonight, I shall drift to sleep with the sound of Hebrews in my ears.

Good choice.

Sunday July 31st

Today is Baptism Sunday at church.

My mind and soul are at the event celebrating and cheering on all those who have made or will make the decision to be baptized. I am praying for everyone who will be involved, from the Pastor to the smallest soul.

My stomach is bubbling. Oh man, I have a savage case of the bubble guts. The contents therein are making its way to the exit sign. No. No. What the what? No.

My butt automatically goes into clench mode.

I jumped up and start the car and peeled off like a bank robber. It's a cat and mouse game that is going on here. I speak to my guts and my butt and ask for patience. The content inside gave me a 5 minutes window. I prayed, "Lord Jesus, help my guts to stop talking so loud and keep my butt muscle strong, amen." I have about 3 minutes left, and my driving speed has increased. "Why not pull off to the side of the road and just drop it?" I thought to myself. Hell no!! Keep driving! Keep driving! My guts start to complain even louder. I began to reason, "Hold strong butt cheeks. Hold the line. You can do this". I have 1 minute and 10 seconds left.

Then I saw a gas station, I hit the turn on two wheels, pulled up, grabbed the car keys, ran towards the back of the store, snatched up a roll of toilet paper and kept pushing forward. There was 14 seconds left. "I am kicking down this door and snatching anybody off this pot if it's in use," I said to myself. There was 5 seconds left. I opened the door, shut the door, lock the door, wiped the seat and oh my God. "DAMN CHEESE!!!" I said out loud. "Damn Cheese!!!"

I left the bathroom feeling clammy and some type of way. I went back to the old spot and took a "5-water bottle with Irish Spring soap" shower. No more cheese after 6:00pm.

Man, this life is no joke. This is real. What I just experience is real. I would not wish this on anyone, friend or foe. I cleaned up the spot I was in and the car and then organized everything that was mine. I leaned on the car hood and looked straight ahead.

"You know, there is someone whose homeless experience is worse than mine. I have groceries, a job, somewhere to lay my head, toiletries, health, my right mind, in a growing relationship with God and ever-increasing faith. When I stop and look at what I just experienced, even with all of that early morning drama, I am still abundantly blessed. Amen self, Amen indeed. Let's go get waffles and celebrate being blessed," I said to myself and off I went.

At work, I was responsible for my entire department and would be by myself on the sales floor. I arrived before time and remained focused. I spoke to 7 specific people today that I know was sent from heaven above by God himself to come and speak words of life to me.

There was an impartation that was given to me by a specific person. She had no idea that what she spoke about was the exact issue that was troubling me. Then there was a lady, who I would later find out is a Pastor, who prayed a specific prayer about where I am in my life and the change that was soon to come. She even mentioned the specific time and day. There were words spoken from another that re-iterated and reminded me about Gods goodness and how obedience changes seasons.

There was another who spoke about the importance of letting go and opening your hands, so you could receive. Then, another who wanted me to know that there is an importance in not staying stuck. I must move forth and go through the opens doors that are for me alone. Man listen, by the end of the night, I was high from all of the "angels" that came to visit me at work today.

It took 3 hours to come down.

After going through all the nighttime routines, I listened to Deuteronomy and felt like I was released into the promise land.

I wondered what this next step that I was about to take would be like.

Monday August 1st

It's August. It's a new month.

Today I am led to a different location for my morning duties. It was to a really nice hotel. Using their bathroom, I took care of my morning responsibilities. After I was done, I sat down in the hotel lobby to relax for a moment. I needed something light that will sustain for hours. Today will be an oatmeal kind of day.

Earlier in the year, I made arrangements to go on a cruise, but I am not feeling like it's time to do that. After a brief call, it was agreed that it would be given away to someone else.

God bless who ever received it.

Last week was a week of forgiveness. It took a toll on me emotionally. I was still drained. I noticed that old remnants tried to linger in my thoughts and bring back old emotions and feelings. "No," I stated out loud. "I am not going back. I am moving ahead. You old dead thing, you were evicted, and I have no desire to allow you to return and dwell within my mind, heart and soul. Your dominion has come to an end. I speak the name of Jesus against you."

I may have my issues with my belief and my trust of God, but my faith in Jesus has grown by leaps and bounds. I know how and when to use His name and apply His blood.

It's time for a visit to the laundry mat.

The conversation with the owner was very inspiring. After folding and putting away my clothes it was time to clean the car, re-adjust items, thoroughly vacuum inside and wash the outside. I was in the mood to read so off to the bookstore I went. As I sat in the car, something in my spirit was not right. I sat still so it can come to me. I thought of my work environment. I was beginning to be affected by the work environment. What was on the outside was beginning to find its way inside. It came through a conversation with a co-worker that was filled with confusion and contempt.

She was toxic and liked to share her thoughts and opinions with whomever slowed down long enough to listen, and she did not care if anyone heard what she said and how she said it.

I prayed for peace. I prayed for peace to have its way in that place today. I prayed that peace would agitate the spirit she was operating in and that healing would find its way to her wounds. After spending time in the book store and then going to replenish my groceries, it was eventually time for work.

It was straight warfare at work.

The manager for that day was a piece of work, a real piece of work. Sometimes I think he forgets that he is dealing with adults. He came after me with a lie that required me confronting him and checking his tone, attitude and behavior. It required all the formal training from my corporate America days and all the discipline of being a believer for me not to release the part of me that was not always saved and knows how to rampage any person. Had grace not strong-armed me, I would have been unemployed. #RealTalk

A customer had a nasty attitude and came in the store being argumentative and combative. She approached me with accusations, agitation and hostility. While she was doing that, I prayed. When I open my mouth to respond I knew what ever came out it was the Holy Spirit because she was quiet, and that nastiness was shut down. #RealTalk

One of my co-workers approached me and said, "Michele, we have got to stay prayed up in this place." I said, "Amen my sister." She mentioned that there seems to be a foul Spirit lurking around today and that her weapon of choice was silence and pleading the blood. The lady that had the issue of agitation and hostility went after the manager also. He put her in place. I simply finished my part of the transaction and walked away with my commission. Amen.

This was the longest day ever.

The manager was agitated and a pain all day. The customers were demanding. Some were kind, and some were not. I was at peace within while there was hostility and upheaval in the environment.

At 8:00pm, I clocked out and left. I was worn out and fatigued. I headed to the local gas mart and prepared for the night ahead. As I sat in the car, I began to doze off in the driver's seat. Man, I felt beat up. My spirit was agitated.

I drove to the same old neighborhood and to the same spot, but something felt different. I circled the neighborhood and came back. Shifting my sleeping position many times, it was an uncomfortable sleep. It was time for the Word.

Tonight, I craved Hebrews. It was the air I needed to breath.

Thank God for the Bible.

DON'T

DIE

IN THE

PROCESS

Tuesday August 2nd

I jumped up in a state of heightened alertness, concerned and ready to fight.

I reached for what I keep on me at all times to protect myself, but this was a dream. No, this was a warning.

In the dream, I was in my car and looked out through the windshield down the road ahead and there was a snake, specifically a black cobra. As I prepared to leave, the snake started to make its way toward me. Then it jumped and lunged at me. But there was a protection in front of me so what came at me simply did not work. In the dream the protection was the car windshield. I had the opportunity to stare this snake in the eyes. I saw what hatred, kill and destruction looked like. I saw what it looks like for something evil to have been sent on assignment to take me out.

I saw it and it saw me.

As I came down from this emotional jolt and started to get my bearings, I tried to start the car, but the wheel would not turn. I got out the car and started to walk. It was time. I prayed and asked God for the specific revelation. He reminded me of Deuteronomy chap 4. It was time to leave. It was time to leave this neighborhood. This was it. Last night was my last night here. I thanked God for what the neighborhood provided me with.

My grandmother always said, "God never destroys a city without first sending a warning." As I looked around, I was reminded that the things that are unseen are more real that the things that are seen.

Thank you, God, for the warning.

I drove out the complex knowing I would not return and not knowing where I was supposed to go. I drove. Made left turns and right turns and stopped at red lights and ended up on the other side of town. There was an upscale hotel on this side of town. As I went in, I took all items needed for my morning clean up. The bathroom is clean, the water is hot, and I am thankful.

As I looked in the mirror, I had no words for me, none. I cleaned up in silence and headed to the gym parking lot.

I needed a deeper stretch this morning, so I added some yoga. It was time for my early morning walk and conversation with God.

"Lord, I may have my struggle with belief and trust in you, but I am grateful that you don't let where I am in my walk with you stop *you* from being committed to me. I am so grateful that you are not like humans. I have some serious things to work out and through.

But, I want to say, from my mouth and heart to your ears, thank you for your protection and commitment to my safety."

I headed to the local Quick Mart for gas, ice and hot water. I cleaned up the car and just sat still. It was time for my personal development call. After the call, I read Deuteronomy chap 4 and started to ask for understanding. Man, what an insight. I was reminded that I am not to become like the inhabitants, that wherever I was, whatever place I am or will be sent, I am to show them God in my attitude, manners, behavior, words and deeds. I am to effect change and not get infected by the ways or what I come in contact with. I was reminded that I am to remember that I am passing through the land and I am not to become distracted by the activities or adopt the influence.

This spoke specifically to the place I currently work.

I felt this overpowering need to pray and man when I tell you I started to pray in tongues and the whole nine. There was such a thick presence in the car that overwhelmed me so much, I could only cry. I felt like there was a cleansing that was happening from the inside. I was refreshed. I felt light and clean. Regrouped and refocused. I could not move to go anywhere, so I sat still.

After a while, I came out the car and inhaled deeply. My lungs held the air as long as it could then I exhaled until there was no air left. Man, what a morning. I checked over my budget and realized that I was missing $4.31. I could not find it.

Dang!

After writing in my journal, I felt the need to see an old friend in the neighborhood. He decided to leave the photography business and move forward.

"Michele, I am now a manager for a HVAC company. It's a job". I looked at the business card he placed in my hand. I did not see any joy in his eyes.

When we spoke about photography, there was usually a glow that came from the inside but now, he looked unsatisfied. "This is where life has pushed me. Now there is no more business and the shop is no more. It's no longer the place for us to meet and talk," he said. There was a longing in his voice. He was packing up the last bit of items from the store and putting it into his car. I watched as he moved and shifted the items in the trunk to make room for more. He was not very talkative and that was not like him at all. His look was more than sad, he looked deeply disappointed.

I walked into the store and looked around. Memories of conversation that I had with him about cameras, lenses, f-stop, computer programs for editing images, mistakes that beginning photographers make, meeting other photographers and listening to their experiences began to replay in my mind. But it was the first conversation we had that was at the forefront of my thoughts.

"Michele," he said to me before I walked out the door "If photography is what you desire to do, you must think like a professional photographer. You must think like a professional".

The store was now in a state of organized confusion. It reminded me of where I am in my life.

"I remember when I first came to Georgia; you were one of the first people I met. You showed me kindness and helped me to grow as a photographer. Thank you for all you did to help me, Hai. I truly appreciate you," I said. We hugged each other and looked at the store one last time.

As he drove away, I saw the disappointment he felt about the decision he had to make concerning his business.

Life events had also occurred to me. Today was the day. It was time. I sent my family a text. The time had come. I am leaving. I looked around and knew that I had reached the end of something here. In this place and in this state, at this moment it was over. There is a journey I am preparing for and this is part of the process. This place of my struggle with my past, functioning broken, living a life of quiet desperation, Lord I believe but help my unbelief, an $8 an hour job, longing for forward progress but returning to backward motions.

No, enough was enough.

I must take this step for me. I must go on this journey to talk to my older brother.

He is out West. There are things in my past that he knows about. There are questions he has answers to. There are experiences in my life that he himself were familiar with because of his own journey. There are answers that are on the other side of fear. The answers are calling for action. The fear was calling for stagnation.

I received a phone call from my sister, a text from my mother and a text from my younger brother. It was time for a family meeting to bring insight and understanding. I headed to the book store to write my thoughts, eat and decompress before it was time to go to work. It was a calm day at work, no drama, no chaos and no mayhem. I spoke to my manager and let her know about some concerns I had. In many ways, I was saying goodbye. It was a slow day. I spent time away from those who were negative and was very careful about the conversations that I was around.

My soul was happy.

The day was quiet. I changed into my comfortable clothes and headed to the quick mart gas station. As I sat there, I was simply waiting. "Lord, where am I to sleep tonight, lead me when you are ready." I started the car and followed the prompting that was in my spirit. I turned right, then left, then left then right then stopped at a light. Then I turned right, then right and then went up the ramp to turn right here.

I was in the parking lot of the upscale hotel I was led to earlier that morning. It was well lit, full of cars and quiet. I looked around. My eyes were looking for any movement.

I turned on Deuteronomy and closed my eyes.

Wednesday August 3rd

It was hard to sleep.

Up every 2 hours, the gorilla was on look out. That was her job, B.O.L.O: Be. On. Look. Out and keep the protection close at hand always. At 6:15, I came off alert and gathered my morning clean up items.

I walked through the double doors of the hotel and said good morning to the front desk clerk. Then I headed to the bathroom and took care of my morning responsibilities. As I came out the bathroom, I noticed that breakfast was being prepared. The buffet was laid, and the fragrance called my name. I strolled in, said good morning to all the early risers and began to help myself.

I grabbed waffles, small box of cereal, turkey links, bagel with cream cheese and seasoned potatoes. Yasssss! My body celebrated. There were lots of repairs that were being done for a local company, so the lobby was full of men in hard hats and jeans with tool belts and loud conversation. However, when they got their breakfast, it was quiet. We nodded at each other as a morning greeting and ate in silence.

After a great breakfast, I took some to-go fruit, thanked the front desk clerk and headed out the door. I got in the car, drove to the gym to stretch.

Then, I cleaned the inside of the car trunk then headed to the Quick Mart gas station. I got ice for my fridge and came back to the gym parking lot. After that, I prayed, participated on my personal development call and simply exhaled. I went to cash my check and found that I had stashed $4.00 in my wallet. I turned around and put it in the hand of the girl that was behind me in the line and said, "God wanted me to bless you with this. He just wants you to know he loves you."

I left and went to pay some bills and got items for my car.

While at the auto shop I had a great conversation with 2 helpful men who worked there, Willie and Bajan. They always make me smile. Our conversation was seasoned with golf, going after your dreams, God, family, taking care of your car, church, and many other topics. We also discussed why social media is destroying more relationships than ever before.

They made sure my car had what it needed before they went back inside to help customers. I received a call from my good friend, Robert. He would check in on me every 2 weeks or so. We always have transparent conversations that last well over an hour.

I headed to the local store to replenish my milk and other perishable items. Then headed to storage to lighten the load and check up on my items. It was a day filled with things done to stay busy and break the monotony.

Night arrived, and I headed to the Hour of Power prayer called Access. My kingdom brother, Irmiyaa, prayed over me. I truly value his fire and passion for God. I spoke with my younger brother about my move out West. He shared his insight, thoughts, concerns and advice.

"I will keep you in prayers. Make sure this is what God wants for you before you go". I thanked him for his love and his prayers. I understood where he was coming from. My mom wanted to set up a family conference call for the coming Sunday. Everyone agreed.

I headed to the gas station, got the needed items and drove to the hotel. In the parking lot, I set up my blanket, pillow and sheet for that night and made sure my morning clean-up items were already set and ready for the following morning.

I was tired of worrying about what could happen. I began to realize that if I focused on what could possibly go wrong, it was unconsciously inviting it into my life. No sir, no sir.

I shifted my thinking, prayed, and rolled onto my bedding.

Thursday August 4th

Today would be different in every way.

I woke up 3 times during the night. Being in this new location still has me on lookout but not on high alert. I guess I must learn to relax as best as I can. Although I know this situation is not ideal, I insist that I will make the best of it.

It was about 6:03 when I decided to head inside the hotel. The outer doors were unlocked but the inner double doors required the room key. I strolled back out and waited for about 15 minutes. Then, I went back in through the doors and went to the bathroom.

For breakfast, I prepared French toast, fruits, croissants and cream cheese. I was not hungry in the moment, but I prepared it for later. I had a tall cup of hot water.

The computer in the lobby was available so I looked around and checked out what was going on in the world of news. I researched flights to Nevada and decided on Southwest Airlines since I never flew with them before.

I left the hotel at about 7:30am. For me that was very late. Then I headed to the gym parking lot for deep stretching and walking. I love to walk. It gives me the chance to talk to God and clear my thoughts. I love talking to God straight from my heart. I tell him everything. I express the depths of my heart's desire, my concerns, aches, despair, disappointments, questions and even my moments of silence. What exactly would I find out West that I could not experience in Georgia? What part of me would I discover in Nevada? Would Nevada build me or destroy me?

Is the climate conducive for my growth?

As I walked, I was reminded that I had begun a process and many parts of my intangible self had begun to die. I learned there is no shame in admitting that I am a believer struggling with lack of trust and un-belief and that this current experience and the one to come was stripping me for greater. There is no shame in accepting that God and faith are deeper in me than I even know.

I know the reason I am going to Nevada and the reason I think I am going to Nevada might not be the same.

This experience that I am in is teaching me to confront fears in my life and in my mind. This going through is to give birth to the next. Because of my acceptance of being a child of God and in learning more about who Jesus, I believe there is more that is required of me. I can feel it.

I am under grace, mercy and favor.

I might not have an apartment or a house, but I am far from homeless. I have shelter, food, clothing, favor, grace and safety. I truly am blessed. There is boldness in confessing I truly am blessed. I had never felt such confidence in being blessed before. I never understood it before. I never saw it before. In this place of being stripped, I have discovered a virtue in the intangible that I never knew existed. I feel complete. Something in me just broke. I connected with something within.

There is a feeling inside of me that shouts, "I can make it no matter what."

I got it now. I am feeling what hope feels like when it goes from being something I have heard, to a concept I think, to a word I speak, to an experience I have, to a place of KNOW.

I KNOW HOPE!

I went to the bank and deposited exactly what would be needed to pay for my phone bill and my one-way ticket to Las Vegas, Nevada. I will be leaving on Monday, September 12, 2016 on Southwest Airlines. I drove to the parking lot of the home repair store and contemplated.

What the hell did I just do? What in the world am I really doing? I felt the fear of the unknown rise within me. It began to explain to me that this would be a great mistake and that I have no idea what is on the other side. Why the west coast? Why so far away? What if you go to the airport and no one comes to meet you? What if you leave everything and you arrive and there is nothing? You don't know what's out there. I let fear run its course until it ran out of scenarios.

"Fear, I have a wonderful feeling that in Nevada, I will discover something that will set me free in a way that no other place can. I will find something, see something, know something, and learn something. Fear, another side of me is on the other side of you and you are not strong enough to cripple me this time. Enough!" I said.

I left the parking lot and drove to the movie theatre. It's time to break my fast.

The fruits and French toast are extremely tasty. I enjoyed it with 2 glasses of cold milk. After my breakfast, it was time to head to the bookstore for reading and writing. I am feeling very hopeful and grateful. I felt more than lucky and for the first time in a long time, I felt worthy of more. My instinct told me there is more that is waiting to happen for me in Nevada.

I spent the bulk of the day in the book store. I looked at travel magazines and began to plan for some of the places I long to travel to. "Yes I can see myself here. I can also see myself there. Yes, I can see myself wearing that, and I can see myself driving that. I can see myself scuba diving in that ocean. Yes, I can see myself like never before," I thought to myself.

It was time for the bookstore to close. Man, the day passed quickly. My mind was lost in the possibilities of a better, greater, whole, well balanced life. I went straight to the hotel parking lot and found a great spot to park. I set up for the night and settled in. My phone battery was low. If I listened to the Word I would run completely dry. I would have to listen to the Word that was hidden in my heart instead.

As I reflect on the day, something is scratching at my thoughts but did not want to reveal itself. There is something here.

Good night, God.

Tomorrow, the unreachable unrevealed thought will make itself known.

Friday August 5th

I can see. I am up early. I made it through the night safely.

I kneeled down on the carpet in the back of the car and prayed and thanked God for giving me grace to make it through the night to see another day.

I went inside the Hotel and started my morning routine. Today's breakfast consisted of waffles, seasoned potatoes, juice and hot water. For later, I prepared bagels, croissants and fruit. Using the computer in the hotel lobby, I researched more about Nevada, listened to the repair guys talk about their different routes for the day, drank my hot water and charged my phone. I leaned back in the chair and exhaled.

After decompressing, it was time to leave.

My favorite place is truly the gym parking lot. I watched many people work on their bodies. I stretched my body and cleaned out the car. After a brief walk, it was time to head to the Quick Mart gas station and got ice for my fridge. I wanted to do some more research, so I headed to the local library.

After about 2 hours, I headed out to the movie theatre. On my way, I brought myself some rice and beans from the local restaurant and decided to marinate in the parking lot. After devouring some good grub, I was in the mood to read. I headed to the book store and read a book called Instincts by TD Jakes. It was getting good. I lost all track of time and had 15 minutes to get to work.

After changing in 5 minutes, I hit the road. Thank God I worked in the neighborhood and arrived with 3 minutes. I headed to work, walking on sunshine.

My day is very interesting. I am watching one of the managers and she is straight suspect right now. She is being nice to me. I don't trust her. I kept myself busy with customers and product placement.

After work, I headed to the book store for hot water and honey. I walked to the car and got all my items and prepared for tomorrow also. It was time to get some ice from the Quick Mart gas station and then I'm off to the hotel parking lot. When I got there, I noticed it was full so I had to park around the back.

As I prepared my bedding and laid down, I felt a sharp pain on my hip on the left side. This pain introduced itself to me the previous year, but I did not follow up to get it checked out. I will head to the hospital on next Wednesday to make sure all is well. I have increased my milk intake.

Perhaps my age is a factor. I don't know.

Well, one thing I don't want to do is fill in the blanks with negative thoughts. I prayed over it and spoke the Word of God over it. The bible clearly states that above all, God wants me to prosper and be in good health, so I will go that extra mile and make sure my health is indeed good.

If God wants health for me, I will want it for myself.

I fell asleep listening to the book of Ezra.

Today was a good day.

Saturday August 6th

Its 4:32am and I am up.

My mind wants to wander on things I have been set free from. All the old junk from my past keeps trying to resurface. I refuse to participate in the thought. It's an early morning fight. Old thoughts about old loves, guilt, frustrations, disappointment about old situation. Nah Bruh, Nah. I will not let my future be held hostage to my past.

I will not start my day mentally climbing out of a hole.

I rolled onto my knees and began to thank God for today. I thanked him for grace and mercy and for caring for me and protecting me while I slept. I sat up and began to put away the bed items. After I finished, I sat still and closed my eyes. Then there were prayers that came from deep within. I have no idea what was being said but the more the words came out the more the thoughts began to die. I thank God for the Holy Spirit who interceded for me. He saved my mind. By the time I was finish praying, I felt as if I were repositioned and replanted in Him.

I came out the car and inhaled deeply. I made it. I made it.

Gathering my things, I went to the hotel bathroom and took care of my morning responsibilities. The water was cool today. My skin appreciated it. For breakfast, I had turkey sausage links, scrambled eggs, gravy, cheese and a biscuit. I set some aside for later also. The lobby was somewhat crowed today. I kept to myself and was very watchful.

When things settled down and the crowd thinned, I logged in on the computer for about an hour. When it was time to leave, I thanked the front desk clerk for her kindness. Since it was so late I cleaned the car and put away all the morning items. I was led to the other side of town today. In the parking lot I organized the trunk and threw out all the old ice that was now water. As I went into the grocery store, I met a young man.

"Hey young man, why are you working so hard?" I asked. He looked at me and said, "Working hard is all I know how to do. I have two jobs and I work hard there also."

"Young man, your parents must be proud of you," I said. He was silent. He was silent for a long while. "Before you walk away, let's touch and agree on 3 things for you. Is that all right?" I spoke what I heard in my Spirit to tell him. I saw him fight back tears. I gave him a hug and told him I was proud of him and completed my shopping.

As I paid, he bagged my groceries, put it in the cart and walked with me outside. He put the bags in the car. As we parted, I asked him his name.

"My name is T. What's your name?" He asked.

"Who me, my name is...On Assignment," I replied. He smiled at me and I smiled at him. He walked away.

"Michele, I think you finally understand," this is what I felt it in my guts. My name was not the focus. Jesus was and so was hope and encouragement. Had I given T my name, it would have taken away his focus from the one who created the moment. I'm on assignment to have Jesus be seen by others. I understand that I am just the vessel. I get it now. More than ever before, I get it. Being homeless is giving me the type of lesson that I was not getting when things were in place. So in this season of being stripped, I learned the lesson of awareness.

I was enjoying the feeling of my new understanding. I was enjoying the feeling of BEING. There was a heightened sense of life. Not one from existing, but from living. Here I am currently, touching and seeing and living a different type of life. It was one that brought the tangible of actuality that I could feel and engage in, instead of the life I was previously living, which was operating on auto pilot.

The library is crowded. While I waited for a computer to become free, I strolled through. Man it had been years since I visited the library. In my youth, a library used to be the spot to go to and sit for hours, read, sneak in food, do homework, giggle with my friends and hear, "Sssshhhhhh," by the librarian.

When the computer became available, it was time to catch up. I checked my social media, responded to some inquiries, filled out some paperwork, sent some feedback, checked in with clients, etc.

After about 2 hours, it was time to eat. I'm in the mood for rice and beans with tuna fish, a salad and an orange soda. The most satisfying thing is when you get what you desire. I was beyond happy. It was time for work.

The day was light for a Saturday.

As I was in the back with some displaced inventory, my co-worker approached me with her thoughts about the manager and how he can be better. She talked about why she feels she is wasting her time being there. Then she started to go on about a disagreement that she had with another coworker. I was not in the mood to entertain anything messy, so I interrupted her and spoke positively about the situation. She walked away in search of someone else to entertain her. She is addicted to drama. For the sake of my peace of mind, I kept our encounters and conversations to a minimum.

After work it was off to the gas convenience stop. I got all needed items for the night, and then headed back to the hotel parking lot. The bedding was laid out on the back seat. It looked welcoming after a long day at work.

I prayed and asked the angels for their protection.

Then I slept.

Sunday August 7th

I'm up. God is still on His throne, and all is well. Thank you, Jesus.

I was gathering my things to head inside the hotel but felt a pull not to. Instead, I went to the other side of town to a local gas station. The bathroom looked and felt grimy. I simply could not. I walked out and headed back to the car. Then I got the urge to check my items that was in storage.

I headed to the storage facility. It was quiet. As I lifted the gate, a warm blast of air and spiders greeted me. I laid an old towel on the floor, placed 2 plastic garbage bags on the towel, got all my items lined up, stripped and poured a bottle of warm water on my skin. Man listen, to my skin, it was a waterfall. I scrubbed my nooks and crannies as the fragrance of Irish Spring filled the area. Then I used 2 bottles to wash away all residues. After I finished, I dried off, got dressed and cleaned up the evidence of my portable shower. The 2 plastic bags were easily disposed of. No fuss. No Mess.

I stepped out the storage unit and my body inhaled and exhaled. I felt very clean and crisp. I leaned on the car and reflected. I used to take stepping into my bathroom, turning on the water, stepping into the tub and letting it run over my skin for granted.

Not anymore. Not after today. I used to take my safety for granted. At any moment someone could have driven by and it could have been a different outcome, but grace and mercy did not allow that. No more taking my safety for granted. Not anymore. Not after today. I took my bed for granted. The place I would just throw myself without a second glance.

Not anymore.

Not after today.

My heart finally understood gratitude and appreciation. In my mind I had the notion of things always being there so I operated from the thought process of, "it's supposed to be there and will always be there." But being stripped was teaching me the type of lessons that only experience can bring and not notions, arguments or logic. "Thank You, God," I thought. This time, those words came from my heart, and they were not just words that fell from my lips because of training.

I was scheduled to work 7 hours today. It was slow in the beginning but after a couple of hours it began to pick up. I know how to keep busy and productive so there was not much interaction with my co-workers today.

I needed that since I was still in that place of searching the many other things arrogance had caused me to take for granted.

The heat in the car had built up and the car needed a moment to cool down. All the windows and doors were down and opened. During this time, I had the family conference call. I shared my heart about leaving and they shared theirs. I heard their concerns. Making the decision to leave is not easy, but it must be done. I chose not to tell them about my current situation.

There were some things that this season of my life was teaching me. There are some awakenings that being on the streets were teaching me. There are some truths I am facing that I never faced before. This chapter, which make up the story of the book of *my* life, was being lived and written. Where I am, is where I needed to be.

The season of being stripped was a needed one for whatever would come next.

After the conference call, I took the time to walk around the car. I laid my hand on it and thank God for the car. It was providing so much for me that I overlooked. When it cooled down, I headed to the gas mart, got my hot water and ice for the cooler and a light snack.

I drove to the hotel and found a great spot to park towards the front entrance between two big utility trucks. Those dudes usually pull out at 7:00am. I set up my blanket and pillow on the back seat, cracked the window and unwind.

As I laid my head on the pillow, I listened to Hosea.

Monday August 8th

It's the beginning of a new week.

As I woke up, I reflected on the conference call I had with my family. I heard my, mother's heart, my sister's heart, my brother's heart and they heard mine. At the end of the call, they prayed for me and covered me in the blood and in Jesus name. I am so grateful that I belong to this Mitchell family. They enhanced my courage.

They said, "If what you need is on the other side of Georgia, go and get it. If your dreams are on the other side of Georgia, go and get it. If you get out there and you find what you are looking for, praise God for it. If you decide it's not for you, remember that your family loves you and you can come back and start over again." I truly like and love my family.

My life is totally in God's hands.

I also reflected on a conversation I had with my co-worker Kourtney. We were conversing about so many things. His hopes, heart desires, church, God, dreams, relationship, his mom and plans for the next season of his life.

I got on my knees in the car. I am scared, excited and emotionally overwhelmed about this next step I am about to take. I am on count down mode and I was ready. I prayed for many intangible things.

Mostly the courage to persevere.

As I drove from one side of town to the other, I listened to Deuteronomy. I headed back to the gas station and to the storage unit. After morning responsibilities were taken care of, it was off to get ice, hot water and gas.

I had a 9-hour work day today so there was not much time for leisurely stretching and much walking. After getting dressed, it was time to head to work.

As the day progressed, my co-worker noticed that my name was not in the system. It would occasionally kick me out the system. If my name was not found, the commissions that were assigned to me would go towards the store. She was diligent in printing receipts and keeping tabs and we worked as a team to ensure what was assigned to me would be mine.

I brought the issue to my manager and made sure we stayed on top of it. As the day progressed, it began to get busy. As I was on lunch, the manager came in and asked me to come help him find an item and price for the customer. I felt the request was unfair and it agitated me because I have been on my feet for 7 hours and taking this half-hour lunch was what I needed at this moment.

I looked at him in stern silence and he said, "It comes with the job". There were 2 words that almost left my lips, but I kept quiet and instead said, "I will be right there". I went out and found the item, and on the way to take it to the register for the customer, she said she was tired of waiting and left.

See, now I wanted to cuss her up and down the street. Instead, I went back to the break room and reheated my food and ate. I was hostile for the rest of the evening but did not unleash it on anyone. My frustrations for my entire situation were playing in my head. Having to be in a position where I had no choice and felt helpless made me feel weak and I am not a fan of weakness. I was on the edge of reason and almost did a verbal drive-by on my manager several times.

After work, I went outside and exhaled. I had not realized I had so much rage in me. I knew it was more than being interrupted at lunch that was eating away at me. It was the fact that my finances were not in a place that put me in a position where I had power and authority and could say, "no," without fear of repercussion for making a decision that benefitted me and inconvenienced them.

In lack, I had no say.

I took a moment before I got behind the wheel to drive. It would not be in any ones best interest for me to drive distracted. After about 10 minutes of accepting where I am financially, I asked myself a couple of questions. "This is not the first time I have been in this position where I have financial lack. It's not the first time I have felt the hurt and degradation of not being better prepared for my future. And, it is not the first time my decisions have left me scraping the bottom of the barrel where desperation has caused me to settle. The only question I have for me is what is wrong with us internally and mentally? How long will we stay in this posture of financial lack? How long will we have lack in many other areas of our life? How long Michele?"

I had no response. I had no come back. I do know that I must leave to get the answer. And so the stage is set. I drove to the gas station, got what was needed, changed and headed to the hotel parking lot. After setting up my bedding, I listened to the book of Acts.

While listening, I began to realize that my current issues took a back seat to what the Apostle Paul went through for the gospel. I have nothing to complain about.

The event that happened at work opened my eyes of understanding for me to see and recognize that I am failing myself.

I have not financially prepared for my future. I have not been improving myself, therefore I have not increased my worth in the job market. I have sailed on old accomplishments and depended on favors and not on hard work. I have not come outside of what was comfortable so I can grow in discomfort. My fears crippled me. I am great at setting goals, but I fell short on the execution of them so there was no accomplishment taking place.

My goals were sitting on the side lines.

"There is something deeper that is hindering me, I must find it. I must go to Nevada to find it. I need to know why. I must understand the why. I must be free from the why. Why? WHY? WHY?"

I cracked the window for some fresh air. The rain began to fall.

I love the rain. I dozed off.

Tuesday August 9th

I woke up to find my pillow was wet.

Somehow during the night, I had shifted position so the only thing that got wet from the rain was the top of the pillow, everything else is dry. My angels were on assignment for real. Thanks angels. It is 5:00am.

I got on my knees and prayed. After I finished, I sat up and began to start folding my sheet and blanket and was about to put them into the plastic bag I use to store them in when I was told to get back on my knees and get low as possible and move to the other side of the back seat.

As soon as I did, one of the utility workers, appeared, strolled to his truck, which I was parked beside. He went into his truck on his passenger side, looked for whatever he came out to look for, smoked his cigarette, closed the door on his passenger side, and went back toward the hotel.

Here I am, in a position of a crouching tiger on the mat in the back seat of my car, with enough light to see and enough shadow to cover me. I was covered under the shadow of the Almighty, in plain sight. I could see but couldn't be seen.

My God! Jesus! That was too close. Then I heard this small voice simply say, "At the end of following instructions and being obedient, is all God has for you to take care of you." It sunk in. It hit home. After 46 years, many conversations with family and friends, warning after warning, countless life experiences and mistakes in abundance, I finally understood it. Being stripped was teaching me the lesson of obeying instructions.

I was so in love with the experience of life, I forgot to remember that some of life's events and experiences do not need to be encountered, and that's why there is a still small voice that guides and leads and protects. He always sees what is coming and brings the instructions or issues the warning. Simply put, there are some things in life one need not engage in or lose just so they can say, "I have lived a full life".

This is why in the bible; Samuel told King Saul in Samuel 15:21, "Behold, to obey is better than sacrifice, and to harken than the fat of rams". (KJV)

After he left, I finished putting away my bedding, brushed my teeth, flossed, did a facial scrub, washed my face, started the car and got in motion to head out. I continued to listen to the book of Acts as I drove. I went to the storage unit and cleaned up with a sense of urgency. After everything was put in its place, I went to get ice for my fridge and hot water.

While eating my breakfast, I am listening the sermon teaching called Legacy: Part I and II. I also listened to a teaching called: Orphan Annie. Talk about delivering the word of God with power and authority, I was blown away by these topics.

It's time for work. As I went in and got my day started, the GM and another manager asked me to join them in the office so we could review the issue of my name being removed from the system and the commission issue.

There is lots of work to do, today. Clothing and footwear items were transferred from our other location and to accommodate them, clothes had to be shifted on the sales floor, the shoes to be restocked and customers still needed help and so much more.

During the gist of the day, the co-worker who is addicted to drama approached me and said, "I heard you told the manager I was stealing your commissions". I looked at her as to say, "What the fuck you talking about". Then she said, "I can see by the look on your face you have no idea what I am talking about, so I know it ain't you." She tried to get into a long conversation, but I excused myself. I was paying close attention to everything and protecting my ears from listening to words that could get deep within me and do me harm.

I left that night with a joy in my heart. This place where I worked was not my final destination but simply a place I was passing through. My need was being met. Like the woman in the bible who had the barrel of oil, when she reached in, there was always enough so her need was always met. My need was being met. I was not to get distracted at all by anything. I embraced my co-workers as they were and simply kept my head down and did my work. I was on assignment for Jesus and I would complete my assignment before I left.

My night's preparation and parking spot was of ease. Everything needed for the morning was on the floor in the front.

Everything needed for the night was in the back.

I listened to the Book of James.

Wednesday August 10th

My eyes were opened. I was safe. I made it till the morning.

There were people beside me in their car also. I don't know if they saw me but I am on my knees and grateful for another day. I lay back down and rolled to my side.

After a few minutes, I got up, brushed my teeth, flossed, scrubbed and washed my face. Then I started my car and left the parking lot. I listened to Jeremiah, or was it, Hosea, or was it James? I am not sure, but I know it fed my soul.

As I arrived at the storage unit, I noticed there was activity lower down. I moved with haste, got showered, dressed, cleaned up and started to prepare for the day.

I had today off and wanted to treat myself. Breakfast was cheese grits, hash browns and biscuits. While I ate, I listened to my personal development call. Then it was time to make my grocery list, cash the check, pay off the big-ticket items I owed and then headed to the local book store.

On the way to the book store, the car ended up at the parking lot of the movie theatre. You know what, I feel like seeing a movie, but I don't feel like paying.

Today I will ask for what I desire. So off I went inside the movie theatre. I rolled up to the ticket agent, introduce myself, told her I am having a wonderful day and I would like to see a movie for free. I asked her if that would be possible and if so who can I speak to for an answer. She looked at me and smiled and she said, "you know what, be my guest today. Since you are having a great day, let's continue it". Wow, just wow! Look at God. The bible said you have not because you ask not. Man the bible has some of life's greatest principles. I don't know whose smile was bigger, hers or mine. I told her I would be right back.

I went to the car and prepared my picnic basket. Food, juice, snacks and a sheet to cover myself. I was ready. I gave her a hug, went in, got a cup of ice and sat in the most comfortable leather recliner I have ever experienced in a movie theatre.

It was a home experience with surround sound and lots of strange people. I saw Jason Bourne and let me tell you, I did not know how much I missed Matt Damon until I saw him back in that role. It was 2 ½ hours of pure adrenaline and adventure.

I came out the movie theatre wanting to do a Jason Bourne marathon.

After the movies, I headed to the hospital. The pain in my hip is starting to have an attitude and it needed attention. It had been one year since it introduced itself to me, and it had become long overdue to be looked at. It began to hurt, especially in the mornings. I don't like filling in the blanks because chances are it would be with some things that were not true, so it was time to find out.

In the hospital, I waited for one hour before I finally saw the doctor. She ordered some tests and finally came back with some news. I was told that I have bursitis. She said that the fluid sack that cushioned my joints is inflamed from too much stretching and bending and activity. I was given a shot in my left butt cheek to help calm down the pain. I was also given a prescription and was on doctor's orders to rest for 4 days straight. She asked me to lie in the hospital bed for a few moments and rest.

Man, I was on a bed. Even though it was the hospital bed and my butt cheek was throbbing from where the needle poked it, it felt like a room at the Hilton. I could not even watch the TV. I fell asleep. After about 3 hours I was dismissed.

As I walked to the car, my hip did not complain. Actually, my sore muscles did not complain. Now that I knew what it was, I could do my part to help myself. While at the hospital, I met Ms. Jenny. She is a believer in Jesus and we had great conversation. We prayed before she left. I truly felt God led me there to meet her and that my daily assignment was complete.

After everything was said and done, I sat in the car and thought to myself, "I wonder if I should stay in the hospital parking lot tonight." Within me it felt like this isn't where I am supposed to be. I exhaled and felt some kind of way, but I follow the instructions because I can relate to the importance of obedience.

As I drove home, I took notice of all the houses, cars and people I drove by. I noticed that life is happening to all of us. The content may be different, but the context is all the same, life.

I stopped and got everything I needed to get me through the night. As I pulled up to the hotel, there was a great spot waiting for me just off to the side. Tonight, I would sleep in the driver's seat. I put it down as low as it would go and stretched out, just like the movie theater experience I enjoyed earlier.

As I settled down, I thought about my father.

Today was his birthday.

He would have been 82 today. He died in December 1, 2012.

He is in heaven and trust me, he is happy. I thank God for all he has taught me. He and my mother were the ones who taught me about faith.

He had stubborn faith and I believe it added years to his life. Cancer may have had his body, but God and Jesus had his heart and mind.

Stubborn faith.

I learned about strength by watching his stubborn faith daily. I told him I loved him very much.

I listened to the book of Joshua as I fell asleep.

I too will have stubborn faith.

Thursday August 11th

Today I woke up. That is half the battle.

It's Thursday August 11th and today is exactly one month that I have been out of the apartment.

I am still here in my right mind and able to do more than function. I am thriving in my current situation. I have learned so many different lessons that the eyes of my understanding were open and could no longer go back to being closed. It is part of my journey. They were tools I was getting for the next half. How could I not love God? The bible states, "And we know that all things work together for good to them that love God, to them who are called according to his purpose." Romans 8:28(KJV)

There is a higher purpose. There is a life that will change because of what I am going through. Someone's eyes will be opened, and another's life will change.

Someone will get closer to Him, and someone else will see Him in their life like never before. Someone will not be afraid to be truthful with Him and speak to Him what is really and truly in their heart. Even if that someone is me, I can truly say, I am blessed to be where I am in my life. Being stripped for greater was teaching me that situations are necessary. Going through a process is necessary. It took this place where I am right now to discover my purpose. Now I have a new respect and regard for my life, so I can help someone else discover and understand their life.

Now I know my life is not in vain.

I thanked God for a safe night's sleep. My hips were not hurting me today. That is real progress. At first, I was not going to fulfill the prescription since I am not a fan of medication, but I was reminded of the importance of following instructions.

After I brushed my teeth, flossed, scrubbed and washed my face, I started the car and drove to the next stop in my morning routine. I usually listened to a bible chapter, but this morning I started to praise God instead. It was loud, rambunctious, full of life, from the heart and I could not stop. It was an overflow of praises and hallelujah.

I took care of my morning duties at the storage. It was a close call, a very close call as a car slowly strolled by. Thank God I was strategic in where I placed my car and where I took care of my responsibilities. As I finished up and cleaned up and prepare the car for the day, I was still in my praise mode.

It was time to get the ice and hot water. To make sure all was set for the day ahead. I ate oatmeal, and then went to the pharmacy to get my prescription filled. While in the pharmacy, had a very honest and insightful conversation with the cashier about gratefulness and speaking life over yourself. After about 15 minutes, I got what was needed, went to the library, wrote and caught up. I completed 2 hours of computer work, ate fruit, took my medication, marinated in the car and simply relaxed.

I called my brother's wife in Nevada and we spoke about 35 minutes. She shared a lot about her and my brother helping people and that things were being prepared for me. She went on about how Nevada is a great environment to grow into the next stage of adult life. I liked her and her straightforwardness.

I sat in the car and had a conversation with myself about the next phase of my adult life. Is it the right decision? Was I running away from something? Was I running towards a better something?

The reason why I am receiving so much of the intangible things in this season of life is because of the vehicle called faith. It is designed to take me to the intangible blessings and pick up all the items along the way that I would need in and for my next.

Many people always quote "We walk by faith and not by sight". However, the question to ask is how many people apply faith AND walk. There are so many other questions that should be asked.

For example, can everyone pay the price of their faith? For their faith? Can everyone walk it out? No matter where it takes them, are they really ready for the mental anguish and emotional upheaval it will bring? Am I? Are they really ready to lose everything? Am I? How much of God do I really want to know? How much of myself do I really want to get to know? Can I ask the heavy honest question? Can I handle the painful honest answers?

What price am I willing to pay for my freedom? My anointing? Am I truly ready to be stripped, even more, for greater because I cannot go into greater as I am?

I cannot take 46 years of a "bondage" mindset into the "land that flows with milk and honey", which also represents a place of opportunity. My mindset and eventually my behavior will pervert, pollute and sabotage the opportunity, and I will bring bondage to freedom.

I must go through the process.

More stripping is forth coming.

I know it.

I don't know how long I was in the parking lot with my thoughts. I don't know how long I was questioning myself and my past about my future, but when I looked up evening began to creep in.

I headed to get the ice and hot water. While marinating I called my mother. She is well, and she is adjusting to life in NC.

Driving to the hotel, my mind was tired from thinking. It had asked every question it could ask for one day. I was mentally spent. After finding a parking spot, I set up my bedding on the front seat and stretched out and covered with my sheet.

Today was a good day.

Friday August 12th

Its 5:59am. Did I really sleep until 5:59am?

Was I just that physically tired or just that much at peace? Was I just that grateful or just that mentally worn out? I am simply going to be thankful for a safe night's rest and a new day of hope. As long as I am alive and breathing there is hope.

I feel revived and refreshed. That was truly the most peaceful night's sleep I have had since I changed my address. I wanted to curl up in the front seat, but I was on a schedule. Things needed to be done by a certain time. The earlier I moved the less people were around and about. Also, I must not fool myself. I never know who is watching. This is the streets after all, and one must always be on look out.

I brushed and flossed and scrubbed and washed and hit the road. The storage area was quiet, but I did not linger in my washing up. After dressing and cleaning up the inside of the car, I cleaned the trunk, threw away the previous night's ice that is now water, and I made sure everything was secure. I also noticed that the trunk is opening and closing without issue. That olive oil is still in full effect.

There are some familiar faces I see at the storage. We greet each other and keep it moving. I am not the only one who is dealing with homelessness. I headed to the local quick mart gas station, got my ice and hot water. I was not much in the mood for breakfast. Some hot water with lemon would be good for now. The gym parking lot had the usual crowd. Stretching and bending did not hurt as much.

The book store called my name and I spent the better part of the morning there.

Then it was off to the library for paperwork pertaining to my student loans. I called my younger brother's wife, Lena. We conversed, and I heard her heart about my leaving. I headed back to the bookstore to read. Today I had bagels and cream cheese and water with honey, lemon and ice. I started to write. I would document this season of my life. I was glad I made the decision to leave.

It was made from a place of hope and not fears.

It's time for work. The day was filled with mundane things. The fillers that make a day go by. I am good at keeping busy but must learn to be better at being productive. I have met some very interesting people since I have been at this job.

One of the managers gave me a compliment; I thanked her and kept busy. I have been awakened. I refuse to be part of the things that are clique related.

After work, I headed to the book store. I wanted to write. Quiet thoughts and unspoken things needed to be written down. I came alive in that environment. I left at around 10:00pm. When I went to the hotel parking lot, I noticed that the utility trucks were gone. Since it was the weekend, all the prime front spots were taken, and the lot was full. They were gone for about 3 days. I pulled up beside a long moving truck that was on my left. I was sleepy and had no control who would be on my right when I woke up. All I could do is apply faith for a good night's sleep.

I listened to the book of Genesis while I was getting the bedding together.

Noah was building an ark and getting ready for what was to come.

Yes Noah, now that's a faith move.

Tonight, I will sleep on the front seat. I was doing my part to stay off sleeping on my hip as much as possible. As a person who slept on her side, it was hard to not roll over and curl up.

I made it another day God.

I held on for one more day.

Saturday August 13th

I woke up and peeked over my dashboard.

There was a police car parked in the next parking section and diagonally in front of my car. He was reading something off of the screen. I eased back down on the front seat and rolled over. My movements were minimal, and I figured that of all the type of cars I want around, surely a police car is a good thing. I went back to sleep.

I heard voices walking in front of my car. A female was on the phone with someone and she was making a very loud point. Loud voices this early in the morning? Really? Her friend became agitated then they began to get loud with each other. They were walking back and forth between my car and the car besides me. Just loud as hell. "Don't get up, just stay where you are," said the still small voice within me. They continued for about 5 more minutes. Then they got in their car and drove away.

"Michele, you are really vulnerable out here. When you sleep, you really are subject to any and everything that can possibly go wrong. Well God, more and more I realize exactly what I am. I am without a home, sleeping in my car and subject to anything. It know it is because of your grace that I am making it. Thank you for covering me and protecting me from things seen and not seen. You protect me when I am awake, and you protect me when I am asleep. You protect the car from all the drama of mechanical things going wrong and spiteful peoples desires to break in and take it. God, just in case you were not told recently, I truly love and value you and thank you for valuing me and teaching me to have more value for myself. Good morning and how are you today?."

I began to pray and thanked God for so much. I was reminded of grace like never before. I was safe while the environment around me was unsafe. This vehicle called faith that I am becoming more acquainted with is priceless. It is taking me to places in my walk with God that I have never been before.

The intangible things are priceless. There are many who are in the same situation, some are better off, and some are worse off.

Thank you, Lord, for all your kindness, and for me being on your mind.

Its 6:00am. I did part one of the morning routine. Then I went off to the other side of town for part two of the morning routine.

My "rain shower" was well needed this morning. I woke up with savage cramps and my monthly visitor. Dang you, period! Dang you, period, as you came upon me while I'm on the streets! Well this is life, this is real. This is what many have experienced. Dang you Georgia for this southern heat and humidity while I have my period! Dang you, period! Dang you, pads with wings! Dang you, period underwear! Dang you, medication! Dang you, Michele, for having no Midol or Tylenol! After about 20 minutes of "dang", I settled into the rest of my routine. Dang you, routine!

I am feeling crabby today. I better keep a low profile.

As I headed out the gate, I noticed that it was open and not closing. I was concerned. That was definitely not cool. Perhaps it's time to take the money I was saving and get a room for a week or so. I am paying close attention.

I went for my ice, hot water, got gas and headed to the gym parking lot for stretching and walking. After I was finished, I read about King Solomon and how he asked God for wisdom to govern His people. It must have been quite a weight that was on his shoulders for his heart to make such a request. I had an incredible desire to pay my tithes. I went to the bank and deposited my tithes then did an electronic payment from my phone. I kept 10% from every check in my wallet but felt the need to pay it today. So glad I obeyed. There was a smile on my heart.

Being obedient was very difficult for me and still is very difficult for me. I am getting better at it but it is hard as heck. The fact is, I was always better at sacrificing than obeying. Lately I have been learning the lesson and seeing the results. I am getting better.

I headed back to the book store and read some more of the book, Instincts by TD Jakes. It truly is amazing that everything we need is already within, yet it takes life events to occur to pull it out.

I went to work and told my manager I would be leaving in about a month. She told me to go get what my heart desires.

I thanked her and encouraged her also go get what God has for her. It was a good day. Many customers gave me lots of hugs and encouragement out of the blue.

For them it was odd, for me it made sense.

After work, I decompressed at the book store. Had some hot soup and a phone conference with Kia and Nikia, 2 ladies on the Hospitality team at church. I needed to make sure that the responsibilities I have in my church would not fall to the floor and things would continue flawlessly when I leave.

They are stepping up as leaders.

The hotel parking lot was full except for the last row all the way in the back. I drove around 3 times just in case someone was pulling out but no such luck.

Dang you, spot in the back!

As I was setting up my bedding more cars pulled up beside me. I was glad they did. They looked like they also needed some rest from a long day's activities. We nodded our greetings and continued what we were each doing.

My hip started to hurt off and on. Unfortunately, I could not take the recommended days off. I still took the medication, but I had to work. With only a couple of weeks left, I wanted to save as much as I could before I left.

I am tired. My body is tired. My mind is tired.

Dang you cramps and tired!

Sunday August 14th

When I woke up, my best male friend from childhood was on my mind.

I began to pray for him and not only him but for my other friends. They were on my heart and mind. I learned years ago that when someone is pressing on my mind and heart, reach out. And if I cannot reach them, I can truly pray for them.

Prayers have no boundaries and no curfew. It can save a life even if that specific person is not physically present. Prayers can protect and save and change anything. It has power beyond comprehension. Prayers will either change a situation or change the way I see and handle a situation.

I prayed for them to have an encounter with God. I asked for them to be saved, rededicated back to Him, and to come into a relationship with Him. I prayed for Godly friends to surround them, for them to find a solid bible-based church, to be part of a strong community of believers, for their future to be different than their past and for forgiveness to be in their hearts.

My heart prayed specifically for Andre, Michelle, Walter, James, Judine, Lorenzo and many others. I prayed for their protection at work and from what is always lurking but can never be seen.

I brushed my teeth, flossed, scrubbed, washed face and pulled out to head to the other side of town for part two of my morning routine. I was led to the local gas station and met the attendant named, "E". I headed to the storage, parked and looked around. My spirit was troubled. Something did not feel right. I got back in the car and headed back to the local gas station. The bathroom was clean, and I did my morning duties there.

After I finished, I went to the car to continue cleaning up, wiping down the seats and dashboard, emptied out the water from the cooler and put away my night clothes. After all was situated, I went inside to speak to "E". I looked him in his eyes and said, "E, what can you tell me about God that will help me make it through today and daily."

He paused looked at me and said, "Faith and Hope sis, daily you must have faith and hope."

As we began to speak, he shared his heart about church, his grandmother's passing, a feeling of being stuck and life passing him by. I asked him for his phone and downloaded our church app and the website. I took him to the message section. I told him to ask the Holy Spirit to guide him to a message to start with and that one of my favorite message series is called, "Jesus Is." He said that when things get slow he now has something to do other than let his mind wander. We said our goodbyes.

I sat in the car and tried to pull together what just happened. These are not coincidences. These are divine appointments. I am literally being led to specific people at appointed times to do what I am purposed to do and say what the Holy Spirit unction's me to say. I am being used for His glory. In the midst of my mess, my lack, my self-inflicted drama and chaos, me not having my life together, God still wants to use me to speak life to someone else. Why use a wretch like me? I am not qualified.

But perhaps, it is not about qualification, perhaps it's about availability and willingness to be brave enough to follow instructions when prompted. And in this moment of being stripped for greater, I realized that a transaction occurs every time I follow His instructions and speak what He tells me to say. That on the other side of my obedience is someone waiting to receive. That they perhaps had a question, or had a concern, or needed encouragement, or needed to know, in that moment, that God has not forgotten about them and that they matter.

They needed to know they are so significant that He would reach out to them through someone like me, the most unqualified person they will probably ever meet. He let me know, that even with my trust issues and belief issues, an everyday person with no title, no savings, no home, struggling in my walk with Him, I can still be used for His glory. Because in the end, it's not about me and my feelings, it's about someone's soul that is on the edge.

It's time for my ice, hot water, stretching and walking. I sat in the car and listen to two messages. The Blueprint: specifically, Courtship and Noble: specifically Character.

I felt the need to walk and pray.

"God, help me as you work on me to be a better person and a stronger Believer. I thank you for all and everything that I am dealing with. I thank you for giving permission for this season of my life to come at me the way it did. I understand that when life events occur, it comes to build my faith and refine my character.

Help me to be more intimate with the Holy Spirit. I know I am going through because of arrogance and pride and disobedience, poor stewardship, bad money management, lack of respect and living life by default. I have not actively participated in my life for many years and then I have the nerve to be jealous of others when they get results for obeying your Holy words and applying your principles to their lives. It is selfish of me to want results but be too lazy to do the work. I am in need of a character upgrade. Thank you for checking me and correcting my character. Again, I ask for your forgiveness for lies and deceptions in so many areas of my life. I pray for an understanding of what is internally wrong. Help me to forgive myself for all I have done wrong to me. Help me to exercise judgment and discernment and understanding and apply Godly wisdom throughout the day and for the rest of my life. It is in Jesus name I pray and ask. Amen."

It is in the long walks that I have the best conversations with Him. As I looked around the parking lot, I thought to myself, "Perhaps my life is not falling apart. Perhaps, it is finally falling into place."

It's time to get to work.

I don't remember much about what happened after this moment.

So, I will end today right here.

Monday August 15th

Its 5:00am and today is so awesome already.

My eyes are opened. I made it safely through the night. My eyes are opened and all is well. I survived.

I feel differently today but I don't know what it is. I don't remember much of yesterday. What happened yesterday? I am still here, so whatever happened, I am still alive. I greeted God, Jesus, the Holy Spirit and the Angels that watch over me.

Yes, I am grateful. I began round one of my morning duties. After that, I was led to the local gas station. That was very odd, but hey, I am not trying to figure out anything. I've noticed that every week or two my location to take care of my morning duties change. The bathroom in this location was clean. The water was hot, and it was early. Usually, most people are getting ready for work in their own homes so there would not be a knock at the door. I went back out, gathered my items and took care of myself.

It was time for the gym parking lot. Today is Monday, so I would be washing my bedding and dirty clothes later. I went through everything and made sure all items were prepared for later. The car was clean, the cooler was emptied of the melted ice, all other items were secured in the trunk and my work clothes were on hangers in the back of the car.

I sat in the car and opened the doors, so it can get some fresh air. I got my bible and sat on the hood of the car. I was taken to Exodus Chapter 16. I read about the Children of Israel, Moses, and how God gave them constant provision and manna. Manna...why am I stuck here in this chapter...Manna? Let me see if I could get this. What am I missing, Holy Spirit? Open my eyes to see it.

Manna, the Children of Israel received bread from Heaven, they named it manna, and God called it bread.

God told Moses that they are to go out each day and gather enough for that day. He provided instructions on how much to take for each person or families' daily need. Each would receive but the amount needed to sustain each person's household would be different.

God told Moses to tell them to gather enough for that day specifically for seeing if they will follow instruction. When He gave instructions to follow, it was to check- the character of the people.

God used the dew to cover the manna early in the morning. What they needed for the day was already prepared even when they could not see it.

When the dew lifted, the manna was there. The tangible evidence of their daily expectation from God and his promise to provide for them had manifested and shown itself.

He honored His promise.

On the sixth day, they were to gather and prepare twice as much because the following day would be the Sabbath, a day of rest.

Some people gathered the manna all the other days and left it until the morning and when they went to eat, it had turned to worms and stank. Some people did not gather twice as much on the sixth day as instructed. When they went out on the seventh day with expectation, they could not find what they anticipated would be there.

And then, BAM, it hit me. Ok, I get it now. It sunk in.

There I am in the bible. That's me. Yep I see me now. I am the one that would have gathered and kept the manna overnight all the other days. That would have been me. And then, I would have the audacity to have an attitude because of the worms and the rowdy fragrance stinking up my tent.

Yup, I am the one that would have gathered manna on the sixth day for the sixth day only, and not have anything to prepare to sustain me on the Sabbath rest day. I am the one that would have gone out on the seventh day to gather. Yup there I am in the bible. All my business on the street! Yup that's me. I would have an attitude with God and blamed Him and shake my fist at Him and yell out, "ITS YOUR FAULT!"

I would not want to admit that arrogance, guilt, shame, and disobedience led me to have a stink tent on all the other days. Nor would I admit to hunger on the seventh day, instead I would simply slip into cover-up mode and say, "I was fasting on the Sabbath anyway." Ego, pride, guilt and shame would not have allowed me to accept that I was in the wrong.

Well damn.

I'm feeling some type of way right now. I got it God. I got it. The instructions yielded the results. Not following instructions yielded the consequences. It was never about the manna, it was always about the instructions.

You know what, I'm just going to raise my hand and then find a seat in the corner with a Dunce cap on my head and face the wall. #RealTalk

I am mentally stuck. I cannot move. I am stuck in revelation processing mode. I must walk. I must walk somewhere around this parking lot. No, I must sit my behind somewhere and let this revelation sink in and dismantle some things in me. No, I can't sit, I must walk. Wait, you know what, I'm just going to stand right here in front of the car like a hood ornament and not move.

Yup. That's what I'm going to do.

I am in awe of God. He was breaking through a lot of old, dead and stagnant ideas and ideology. He was breaking through an old mindset and understanding in my life. These new experiences gave me a new respect, perspective and appreciation for Him and His word. He *is* real. He is more real than what can be seen. Man, listen when you ask for revelation. It's best to ask for strength and mental fortitude to handle it because one thing I know for sure is this, when you get into a relationship with God, He will start to show you yourself!

This revelation cut me deep. My mind was in shock and my body was frozen. In that moment, I stopped looking out of a window and started to look into a mirror.

My mind was hurting. I felt like surgery was happening in my brain. This was a deep cut and it was painful. The truth of who I am was sinking in. In that moment, I saw my whole life, and I saw the mess that it was because of many years of disobedience.

I took out my bedding. I needed to sleep.

When I woke up, I was drenched with sweat. I went to the laundry and washed everything that was dirty. I was still stuck on what I had finally understood about myself. The question I asked myself was why? This can easily be labeled as rebellion but it's more than that. I need to find the source. I need to understand the who and the why.

It was time for work and I did not feel like being there, but responsibility is not about feelings. The workday was good. While there, I met a young lady who is a hair dresser. Her mom had passed, and she was looking for a dress to bury her in. We spoke about her mother, accepting the call of God on her life, belonging to Jesus, her next step in her career and then we prayed.

I also met Ms. S. She shared her heart with me about the prayer of Jabez, about the timing of taking territory, how to treat people, how to handle the responsibility of the word of God and that I need to treat myself to more.

After work I was in the mood to check out social media. I headed to the Quick Mart gas station, got all I would need for the night and headed to the hotel parking lot.

The parking lot was packed but I found a space. Beside me there was a truck with tinted windows.

I had an uncomfortable feeling and started the car and drove out. Drove around for a while and finally there was a spot that opened in the front. I was watching everything. I saw the truck with the tinted windows drive out.

Go to sleep Michele, you are protected.

Well, on that note, off to sleep I went.

Tuesday August 16th

The last thing I remember listening to was Genesis chapter 18.

My hip started hurting more than before. The medication was working but when it wore off, my hip pain was even louder. I needed to stop sleeping on it or do a better job of supporting it for when I sleep.

My friends were on my heart and my mind again. They have been on my mind a lot lately. James, Jamel, Michelle, Walter, and Judine were all on my mind. "Lord wherever they are, whatever they are a part of, whatever is happening in their life, save their lives," I said. I was lying on the back seat and it was after 5:00am. I needed to reach out to the ones I can find. They needed to know they are loved. I thanked God for another day of grace.

It's time for part one of my morning routine.

After the face washing and teeth brushing, I headed to the local gas station. It's 3 minutes from the hotel parking lot I pulled out from. I gathered my items and said good morning to the attendant. The bathroom was clean and spotless. The water was hot, and I was taking a long time just relishing the moment. I had a gut check remind me that this is a public bathroom and to put some hustle in my butt and not forget where I am and to keep my eyes open. When I was finished, I made sure the bathroom looked just like I found it. I asked the attendant his name. "My name is Syed," he replied. I thanked him for his kindness and left.

The gym parking lot was kind of scarce today. Maybe I was early. I did my walking and stretching. Personal development was heavy today, it lined up with what I read in Genesis. I had a hunger and read Matthew Chapter 6. I went for a walk. Someone was in my heart. I had to make sure this was not a distraction or pity. I am not emotionally stuck, I am emotionally longing. I felt that what was, should not be an indication of what can still be. Time does not equal change if acceptance of one's self is not embraced and truth of one's past is not examined.

The fact is that truth and deception cannot co-exist.

I MUST choose.

Choice will bring pain, especially if truth is the most valuable asset needed for me to be set free. Until there is a confrontation and I see the truth, I will linger in what is false. I had to see it for myself. He told me the time will come where I will see the truth of him for myself. God knows me well enough.

I had an urge to look up the definition of deception. I had a feeling that I was standing in my way and needed to move forward.

I went to the library. I was about to do some work when I felt the strong pull to watch a video by TD Jakes called, "Ye know not what you ask." That video lined up with my earlier conversation and request that I had in my heart. That video led me to consider whether I really understood the cost of what I want. Am I ready to get what I want? Am I ready to handle what I want? Does what I want and who I long for really want me? Do I really understand that being in a relationship with God changes everything from the inside out? Do I really understand what grace and mercy does in a believer's life?

Here is what was said in the video about Grace. "There is discomfort in Grace. In grace, when you want something removed, and God says, "My grace is sufficient in that area," It does not mean you don't hurt, don't bruise, and don't cry. Grace just means you don't die. It says that while you are going through, or dealing with the process, some kind of way, you keep putting one foot in front of the other. Despite the issue, you keep going".

"Lord, I thank you for leading me to this video. I thank you for awakening my understanding of Grace, your grace. I have gotten exactly what I needed to keep pushing and going. In this current situation that I am in, being without has caused me to see your grace like never before. Thank you for giving me grace to come back to you on bended knee before it was too late. In the process of me being stripped, I can see your Grace".

After the video, I wanted to understand deception.

I found an article that brought it home for me. "Deception includes several types of communication or omission of communication that serve to distort or omit the complete truth. Examples of deception range from false statements to misleading claims in which relevant information is omitted, leading the receiver to infer false conclusions. Deception itself is intentionally managing verbal and/or nonverbal messages so that the receiver of the message will believe something that <u>the messenger knows </u>is false.

Intent is critical with regard to deception. Intent differentiates between deception and an honest mistake."

Well damn. There it is. Between Wikipedia, Dictionary.com and academicroom.com/topics/what-is-deception, I began to have more understanding about the different types of deception.

I had never read it that way before. This excerpt brought clarity and understanding.

And with this understanding, I was jacked up again.

Deception is beyond toxic and dangerous. It's like inviting someone to swim in a chemical mixture of anger, jealousy, sabotage, envy, hatred and evil knowing it is not good for their health and attempting to convince them it's good for their skin.

It is the fragrance of the enemy.

Deception tumbled the whole world.

As I ate my lunch, I was jacked up. My eyes had been open to the spirit that this man who is on my heart is operating in and with. I was reminded that he is not ready to come out of being deceptive because he does not see the harm he is causing to those he deceives. When confronted, he justifies, deflects and blames. That is the danger that will harm me if I draw close.

It is time for work.

I had a good night. Sales were not bad for a Tuesday. After work, I headed for the usual quick mart gas station. The parking lot was full. I parked in a new spot and I did not like it. I was truly uncomfortable. It was about 11:00pm and I was fidgeting. I would doze off then jump back up.

I turned on my bible app and listened to a scripture.

I found great comfort in it. I began to relax. I know that I am being watched over and I took great comfort in that also.

I adjusted myself on the back seat and fell asleep.

Wednesday August 17th

Its 6:03 am and I overslept.

What the what? I actually overslept. Man, I guess this is what happens when I let God do what He does. I cannot be awake watching over me and asleep at the same time.

I went to the gas station to take care of morning duties first. Upon coming out the store, there was a car that was parked one spot away from me. He was waiting while his friend went into the store. A person came out of nowhere and walked by him and asked him a random question. Then this person stopped and started to fidget. I was on high alert.

Now usually I would get myself together, but I had a sense of urgency to leave. The person passed by the back of my car and I watched him as he disappeared. He kept walking away and looking back at me at the same time. I kept eye contact until he turned away. I tossed my items in the car and headed behind the wheel. When I started the car, I looked back, and the trunk was open. As I came out and closed the trunk this person started to approach the car. I made it into the car, slammed the door and reversed. As I looked back it was coming after me and was steps away from the trunk. I began to pray and at the same time I reached for what I always keep on me.

The gorilla wanted to come out and beat this person but a wiser side prevailed. As I drove away I almost hit a car that made a last-minute turn. I looked through the rear-view mirror and saw that it was no longer chasing me. As a matter of fact, I did not see evidence of it at all. I arrived at the gym parking lot and got out the car and tried to put two and two together.

I read my bible, Matthew Chapter 6. What was that I just encountered? What type of entity was that? Was it a demon? Was it a homeless man that had mental issues? Whatever it was, and only God knows, I am grateful that I was safe from harm. It was the reminder that jolted me back to reality. This is not a joke or a fantasy. I am homeless, and these streets are dangerous. PERIOD. There is danger and potential trouble lurking and it is real.

PERIOD!

Years earlier, I was taught about B.O.L.O by my younger brother Philip. "Meesh, you gotta be on look out at all times, ALL times. Take it from this former knucklehead, BOLO at all times".

Steal, kill and destroy is real. Thank you, Jesus for allowing me to see this person with my own eyes. Demonic possession is real.

I stayed close to the car for a few hours. Then I walked, stretched, listened to my personal development call, and then headed to the quick mart gas station for ice and hot water. I was in the mood for a good book, so I headed to the local book store, found a table, took out my lunch and read for the rest of the afternoon.

I began to feel hungry for prayers so off I went to Access, our prayer hour of power. Let me tell you something. There are some things, that when you go through it, you need the strength of the people around to keep you together and pray with you and for you. I received solid prayers from my Kingdom brothers and sisters. They held me and prayed. They shed tears with me and prayed. Some just came and held me and prayed.

My sister in Christ, Courtney, prayed a most powerful prophetic prayer over me. Everything she prayed touched every area of my life. Access was a safe place for me to fall apart because I would get put back together with prayers. I prayed for my friends and their walk with God. I wonder if they knew how much I love and value them. Before we dismissed, Pastor closed us with the word rest. He spoke on the importance of getting rest. I realized that what he said was for me.

When I left, I conversed with my brother and my sister. As I drove away, I noticed something on the windshield. As I took a closer look, it was a big water bug that decided to crawl and introduce itself to me on the outside of the car. That was all the motivation I needed. I was not spending the night in the car, I would get rest elsewhere. I called another sister in Christ, Whitney, and she opened her door and her home for me to get some rest that night.

The most memorable thing I did that night was take a hot shower. My God, hot running water is the most delicious thing in the world. Having it run over my face and cascade over my body was the most joyful of feeling. Steam on a mirror was the most beautiful of sights. I looked in the mirror and saw me. We smiled at us.

Life is beautiful.

I enjoyed a warm cheese sandwich, some chips, hot cup of tea, a cozy couch and a restful night's sleep.

Thursday August 18th

I woke up and stretched.

I thanked God for His goodness. I thanked him that He shows himself through people. It was time for my exercise, then a shower and then listened to personal development. I was worried about my car. I was like a worried parent. I kept looking through the key hole to make sure he was alright.

I thanked my Kingdom sister for her kindness and headed out the door. When I saw my car, I smiled. My heart was glad. I did not realize that I bonded with my car like I had. After putting my overnight items away, I went to the local Walmart. I needed a new cooler. As I came out, a man holding a bucket approached me and asked for a donation. I had this strange feeling, so I interviewed him to get insight about his motivation because what he was advertising as the reason on the bucket did not feel right. I asked him a couple of questions and he revealed his true self. I am learning to trust me like never before.

After he left, I set up my new cooler. To keep the ice as long as possible, I placed the cooler inside 2 black plastic garbage bags and tied it up. Then I headed to get ice, an oil change and then went to the Dollar store.

I put my mail on hold and went to get it from the post office. Within that mail, there was a check from the power company.

Look at God!

For lunch, I had seasoned lime rice, beans, barbeque tuna fish and a tall bottle of cold water that came from my 2 plastic bag covered fridge. As I ate, I looked around and was grateful. I liked eating in the car with the door opened. After lunch, I went to the local bookstore to read and write. I called and spoke to my sister and my nieces and nephews. They would soon begin their new school year, in a new school with new adventures. They were excited.

I spent the day reading and writing and thinking. The book store was closing. Wait, what? Its 10:00 already. Where did the day go? I headed out to the parking lot with the others. After getting out all the items I would need for the night and the morning, it was time to head to the hotel parking lot.

As I drove past, I saw someone lingering in the parking lot. I made a turn and continued towards another location. When I arrived at the other location, I was truly uncomfortable so I drove through and headed back towards the hotel.

I felt that was where I was supposed to be until further notice. As I drove up, a car was pulling out of a prime spot to the front. Yes, following instructions does yield results, thanks God.

After setting up the bedding and putting things within arm's reach, I went to the back seat and laid my head on the pillow. I looked up to the ceiling of the car. I am truly tired. Not the tired that comes from fatigued, but the tired that comes from having enough.

It's more than being fed up. This feeling of tiredness is a combination of fed up and, finally aware of being fed up and, had enough of myself and my life as it was. It's the fed up that tells you, "We must decide to take action." It's when you are existing, and you have no desire to exist in "existing".

There is a mental block somewhere. There is stagnation in my mind somewhere.

The only thing that is keeping me sane and putting one foot in front of the other on a daily basis is grace and this new level of faith that I am growing in. My father's example of faith that kept him going has transferred to me. My mother's appreciation for prayers has transferred to me. I have come to realize that in this season of being stripped for greater, the intangible gifts that has been the foundation of strength for my parents, has become a significant part of me keeping my sanity.

I missed my father like never before.

Damn I hate tears on my cheeks.

I fell asleep listening to Matthew.

Friday August 19th

It's Friday morning.

I am one week closer to the time when I would be leaving.

The night became the morning. My shoulder began to ache. 3 years earlier, I was involved in a car accident that left me badly shaken up. My shoulder has a hair line fracture that aches like hell and my job is aggravating it. I do strengthening exercises that are non-weight bearing to help it heal. I have to learn how to swim. That's on my "to do" list for next year.

I have been dreaming again. They are vivid, detailed and relevant dreams. Dreams that are so real that for one instance, the details of the dream would come to pass.

"I don't want a mindset of poverty any longer." Wait, where did that thought come from? I no longer see the honor in it. Did I take a vow of poverty to prove I am a child of God? If I have wealth, does that prove I don't love God? I am having conflicting feelings about wealth and poverty. There are some old doctrines that are in conflict with my new experiences.

Living life had circumcised me. This experience had circumcised me. There was a guilt I had about having and there was a frustration I felt for not having. Was I

170

unknowingly sabotaging myself when I had? Was I afraid to have? Who told me that having more means needing God less?

This is too heavy to be thinking about at 5 o'clock in the morning.

The routine had started, brush, floss, scrub, wash, off to the gas station to wash up, move with haste, put away items, clean car, and then get ice and hot water. Once that's done, off to the gym parking lot, stretch, walk, then some personal development and breakfast.

I listen to the book of Acts.

Let me tell you something, the Apostle Paul, who was once Saul who met Jesus on the road to Damascus, was hand chosen by Jesus himself to do the work for the gospel. That encounter changed his destiny forever. That dude survived some things that would have killed him had he not be empowered from on High and mentally tough.

As I drove through the neighborhood, my mind was stuck on something that was said on the personal development call earlier in the week. One of the speakers said, "We have a tendency to host thoughts that lead to behaviors that lead to our demise. We must decide to stop being a welcoming host to things that do not yield positive results and get rid of hosting what have become comfortable thoughts of mediocrity. You can either be a host to God or a hostage to your ego." (Edging God Out)

I headed to the library. When I arrived it was closed, so I headed back to the book store. I looked up the definition of the word host. Host: *a person who receives or entertains other people as guest; an animal or plant on or in which a parasite or commensal organism lives.*

So now, I had to look up the definition of the word parasite.

Parasite: *an organism that lives in or on another organism (its host) and benefits by deriving nutrients at the host's expense; a person who receives support, advantage, or the like, from another/others without giving any useful or proper return, as one wh o lives on the hospitality of others;*
(In ancient Greece) a person who received free meals i n return for
amusing or impudent conversation, flattering remark s, etc.

Wait a fucking minute, are you telling me that some of my thoughts are eating away at me and killing me from the inside? Regulating why I can't or have me believing that I can't? That also explains what I have been to my family and friends on several occasions because of bad decisions and poor judgment.

There was something else that was scratching the back of my mind about my thoughts. I just did not have the words or alertness to identify what it was.

I went to the Mexican restaurant for beans and rice then to another location to eat and think. "The second half of my life cannot and will not be like this. I know exactly what must be done and I am more determined now than ever. This trip will be more than just catching up. This will be about finding out and getting freedom," I said to myself. It was time to clean up and head to work.

I told the general manager about my departure. He was disappointed, but he understood. The co-worker that was addicted to drama approached me during the day to tell me she was leaving on the upcoming Sunday. I congratulated her for her decision and wished her luck for what her next will be.

The day was over at 7:00pm but I stayed in the parking lot for 2 hours. Doing what? I truly don't know. I left at 9:00pm.

I went to get hot water and ice. I ate raisin bread and had hot water with honey. I had a savage case of bubble guts yet again. Dang you bubble guts! Dang you!

I got everything that is needed and headed to the car. After setting up for the night and the morning, it was time to head to the hotel parking lot.

There were 2 spots a little ways off of the front. I did not like it at all but everywhere else was full. Then a 4x4 pulled up and squeezed in besides my car. He and his companion talked for an hour. I dozed off and on while they spoke. Finally, they pulled off and went their way.

I prayed and thanked God for today's grace and mercy.

Saturday August 20th

Its 5:00am. It's early. It's Saturday.

It's dark, I'm tired and I want to sleep. Maybe I could sleep late and do the clean-up stuff a little later like when the sun comes up. It sounded like a great plan to me. "Michele, pull the seat up and then slide all the way to the floor," I heard a small voice say, so I followed the instructions.

Then as I was sliding to sit down on the carpet of the front passenger side, I saw a police car. It came from around the back and stopped one car before mine. He then stayed in his car and shined the bright search light into the car that was parked besides me. He continued to drive and shine his light into all the cars on that row, including mine.

"Oh My GOD!!! Thank you, Jesus, Thank You, Holy Spirit!". I was on the floor in stealth mode. I would have been caught. Probably with my mouth wide open as I slept. "God, you sure are committed to me, thank you." Soon I heard a car drive off and I peeked out the window. It was indeed the police car. After waiting for about 5 minutes, I started the morning routine.

I noticed that my hip is not hurting. I had cut back on the amount of bending and stretching at the job. I believe that it would play a part in helping preserve the integrity of my hip. When I arrived at the gym parking lot, I listened to Joshua chapter 1. When it was finished, I read Proverbs chapters 3 and 5. After my prayer breakfast, I was in the mood for seasoned potatoes, fried eggs, toast and chopped chicken. Instead, I had raisin bread, cream cheese and 2 cups of milk. I had to stay on my budget. I was satisfied with knowing my appetite did not take me out.

At the book store, I was reading a book called, *The Other Wes Moore*. It is an awesome read. My mom called. She let me know her thoughts and what was on her heart. I am surrounded by love and I value and appreciate her.

At work, the day is good and it went by fast. I was helping a woman and we connected immediately. We conversed about lots of things. She spoke words of life to me. Everything she touched on was timely. I left work mentally lighter than how I went in.

In a couple of weeks, I would be seeing my older brother. I have not seen him in 29 years. I could not wait to get to know him. Who was he? What had he been through? What did he learn? He was always smart and well informed and ahead of his time. Actually, he was brilliant. I had wanted to be like him in so many ways.

I wondered if he knows God. I wondered if he knows Jesus. I wonder what our conversations would be like. Well, soon and very soon I would no longer have to wonder.

It was raining. I totally love the rain. I checked in with my brother and his wife in Nevada and let them know I was ok. I was looking forward to finding out what life in Nevada would be like.

After finding a spot to park, I began to unwind. I was more at peace with myself, my current situation and with the knowledge that I will not stay how I currently am. On the other side of this decision, I would get my answers.

I covered myself in prayer and listened to the book of John.

FAKE IT TILL

YOU MAKE IT

HAS COME TO

AN END

Sunday August 21st

I woke up and my mind was empty. No rowdy thoughts.

I woke up early about 2:00am, looked around and went back to sleep. Jumped up at 4:28am, looked around again and saw all was well. I began to talk to God and tell him what was on my heart. I told Him about my concerns, about where I am in my life now, and how I am looking forward to my next season. I told Him that I was grateful that I am able to hear Him clearly. I told Him that I liked Him a lot.

I think I heard a smile in my heart.

I am looking forward to going out West. I am so grateful that the opportunity was offered to me. "Sis, all you have to do is come and everything else would be taken care of," is what my brother said to me.

I went to the local gas station and said hello to Syed. He was very gracious. After all my nooks and crannies were Irish Spring fresh, on the way out, I spoke with Syed. He had big plans for his life and said, "I am working here because I'm paying my dues until such time." It's amazing how much we had in common.

I headed in a different direction this morning and drove passed a diner. Today I would treat myself. I had hash browns, scrambled eggs, biscuit, cheese and grits all for under $3.65. Yes! I found a deal. I headed to Quick Mart gas station, sat in my car and ate. I started to see some familiar faces. The folks inside recognized me and started to call me "the hot water and ice girl".

I headed to the gym parking lot and listened to a message on the podcast. I felt a strong desire to read the bible. Today would be Corinthians 1 and 2 (KJV), Thessalonian and Romans (KJV). The bible is food for the soul and I was full.

It was time for work.

I did an 11:45 to 7pm Sunday shift. My body was tired, and my hip wanted for me to be still. I did not do much bending. It was a slow Sunday, and that is a great thing. "Michele, you must sell. A customer that buys is good for everyone" said the Sunday manager. "Yes, you are right" I responded.

At 7:00 my day was over. I took about an hour to organize my items and get ready for the night. The car is a hot box, so the doors are wide open. I went to the gas stop to get my ice and hot water. The plastic bags wrapped around the cooler were working really well; the ice was not melting as fast. I was hesitant to go to the hotel parking lot. I did not know why. I drove in and 2 minutes later, a great spot opened up towards the front.

There were not many cars tonight.

I noticed that my clothes were fitting me with much room. The last time I weigh myself I was 134.6 lbs. I went from 152 to 134.6 lbs. Well, considering my current situation, I understood.

I went to sleep a whole lot earlier than I normally do.

The last thing I remembered was 9:45pm.

Monday August 22nd

I was out at 9:45pm then up at 12:30am.

Then back to sleep and then up at 3:15am. I was out and then up at 5:02am. My body is arriving at the point where it is ready to sleep for about 3 days. If God was not with me, I would have collapsed a long time ago.

I woke up with God on my mind. I wondered how He was doing. I wondered if I disappointed Him. I wondered how things were with my father and my ancestors. I wondered how Jesus was doing. I begin to pray, "Lord, I pray all is well with you. I am keeping you in my prayers today. I truly love you and value you like never before. If you were not with me, I would have collapsed a long time ago, thank you".

Lately Thessalonians, Romans and Acts have been on my heart and in my mind. My ears and my soul were satisfied when I heard them. My Spirit was rejoicing in the understanding that the simple act of spending time in the bible and learning about God was the best gift I could give myself.

I was satisfied beyond words.

I don't feel like going to the local gas station by the hotel anymore.

I headed to the 24-hour Kroger's grocery store instead. It is early, it is dark outside it is different.

Wait a minute, this is a new week. Wow, I was being led to a new place. Well when it comes to faith in God, there is no routine. It's simply trust and obey. Wait a minute, did I just use the words trust and obey in the same sentence with God!!!! Uh Oh Michele, is it possible that you are becoming more dependent on God and relaxing in the fact that you might be breaking free of your unbelief and lack of trust issues?

Is it possible that you said those words from your heart because God is winning you over by what He is doing for you daily? Winning you over simply because of WHO HE IS? Winning you over through the bible and his Word? Winning you over because you finally trust him? Wait, I think my heart just skipped a beat.

I took a plastic bag and filled it with my morning items and headed to the bathroom. At that hour of the morning, there were very few people that were getting their grocery items. I said good morning to the guard and the cashiers. As I walked, I saw that the overnight workers were restocking shelves and there is cleaning of the floors and preparation for the bakery area is beginning.

The bathroom is bigger, well-lit and clean. I looked around and started my routine. I did not get caught up because no matter what, it is a public bathroom and the public had been in it and will be using it soon enough. It was an Irish Spring rain bath type of morning and I walked out with pep. Since I was there, I might as well get some fruits, grapes, bananas, apples and peaches. Peaches were my favorite food item.

I headed to the local gas stop to get my ice and hot water. I decided to sit in the parking lot and watch the activities of those who have an early morning commute to work. Coffee is the number one item that was purchased. There is construction right across from the parking lot and the workers are beginning to come in. There are cars pulling up to the pump and leaving. It is Monday morning life. My meal for the day is grapes and bananas with hot tea.

After about 2 hours, I drove off and headed to the local Walmart parking lot. I watched someone jogging and felt envious. I always wanted to jog but there were lots of excuses why I did not start. I sat, waiting for the laundry to open which is usually around 7:30 or 8:00am. After the wash, dry and fold, I headed to the DMV parking lot.

It was closer to my job and I would soon have to be there.

Monday mornings were slow, so I worked on some displays and garment.

In the afternoon, I assisted as needed and spoke to my co-worker about some things that were on my heart. I saw that it hit home for him. We spoke about relationships and expectations. I think he received what he needed from the conversation. It was a light and joyous day for me. The new routine had given me a new perspective. Also, I had never woke up thinking about God before. Not to such a magnitude.

I had never prayed for God before. I wonder if He thought I was losing my sanity.

After work, I packed up my items and headed to my refresh stop and then to the hotel parking lot. There are 2 spots left in the entire parking lot. I believe I chose the right one. With the tiredness, it was getting easier to fall asleep. I did not have any energy to do anything but lean the front seat back and cover up with a sheet.

I prayed and turned on the bible app.

God's got this.

YOU CANNOT SOLVE YOUR PROBLEMS WITH WISHFUL THINKING

Tuesday August 23rd

I went to sleep about 9:40pm and was up at 12:30am. Then I was out and back up at 4:28am.

I noticed that today, God was on my mind again. I wondered what He was doing and how life was up in heaven. What did He do all day? I prayed to Him and I prayed for Him. At first it was kind of strange to me. It felt weird actually to pray for God, but I had the simplest of thoughts that made perfect sense. Think about it. If you were in a relationship with someone you love, wouldn't you want that person to pray for you, check in on you and see how you were doing? Wouldn't you want someone to smile when they thought about you?

Uh Oh. This was beginning to feel like a relationship and it was very real. Well, I do know that I like Him very much. Very much.

I brushed, flossed, scrubbed and washed my face. I had my mind on Him and then I pulled out the parking lot and headed to the Kroger. It's late. It was 5:31am.

It's gas station time and all that came with it. I was grateful for this week's change in the routine. I received a text from my younger brother that was very encouraging. I was texting him back when I had an unusual feeling that came from my gut. Then someone pulled up beside me that had me feeling some type of way for real. I started the car and headed to the other side of the parking lot. I finished texting my brother. I enjoyed the hot water and wrote while sitting in the car. The construction workers were beginning to arrive. Some went for coffee and others went to work. I truly love watching men work. I admire men who have great work ethics and know that providing and protecting is what they do.

"Manhood 101: providing for those we love and protecting those we love is what a man does," as my good friend, James, has said on several occasions.

As I wrote, a truck came to drop off items for the workers. He pulled into the site and on the back of the truck are the words Philippians 4:13. A bible verse? For me? Really? That's God talking to me right there, I recognized one of the ways he communicates. I am not one of those people who can quote scripture just like that. I have a few that are part of my arsenal and I know them off the top of my head, but this was not one of them.

After finding it in the bible, this is what it said, "I can do all things through Christ which strengthens me." (KJV)

I had to read the whole chapter. The reason why Paul could rejoice in the Lord, the reason why Paul could say, "Whatever state I am in, I can be content," is because of the strength he received through Christ. Paul had an encounter with Jesus, and that encounter changed his life forever. He knew who's he was and that the person he belonged to really did exist. He knew, and knowing erases doubt.

It takes strength to go through and not lose your mind. Drama, mayhem, chaos and life events came my way, as it is supposed to do, but if I didn't have a core that is solid in the things of God, even while questioning my beliefs and trust, I would have lost hope.

I would have lost my mind and quite possibly my will to live.

Oh my God. Wait a minute. Did I just see myself in the bible again? The encounter Paul had on the road to Damascus opened his eyes in more ways than one. He received more than just his eyesight, he received his assignment. Am I in my "Road to Damascus" encounter in this season?

In being stripped for greater, I am receiving the life changing lesson of knowing who I belong to. It will be engraved in my soul.

After about an hour of sitting and letting that sink in, I headed to the pawn shop to take out a very important item, then to storage to secure the item. Afterwards, a Chick-fil-a chicken sandwich called my name along with some mixed lemon and seasoned rice from the Mexican restaurant. It was accompanied with a cold sprite from my fridge.

Lunch was good.

It was time to head to the library.

Today was the day to type up my letter of resignation. Then a phone call to my younger brother, a group text to the ministry leaders about my transition, off to the book store and finally off to work.

I gave my manager the letter of resignation. She seemed to be distant. I passed it to the GM. He accepted it. It was 9:15pm when I left and headed straight to the gas station. I stayed there for about an hour. When I pulled up all the front spaces were gone, and I did not feel comfortable with the spaces in the back.

I pulled out and went around one more time. Then I saw someone heading towards their car that had a prime front spot. Look at the goodness of God.

I am restless.

Not in the mood for sleeping on the back seat. Not in the mood for sleeping on the front seat. I longed for the simple pleasure of a bed to stretch out in.

It will soon come.

I fell asleep listening to the book of Timothy.

Wednesday August 24th

I love the stillness of the morning. Hello God.

I woke up at 1:00am, then 3:00am and then 4:03am. I started my routine of brush, floss, scrub and wash and prayer. I left the parking lot and headed to Kroger. The bathroom was clean, and it was available.

After my morning responsibilities, I got some fruit, greeted the overnight crew, greeted the security guard and headed to the parking lot. On the way to the gas station, the roads were quiet, and all the lights were green, it would definitely be a good day.

I enjoyed some hot water with lemon and an apple. The noise level started to rise as the sun started to rise. Cars were coming and going, construction, horns beeping, some people talking loudly. Yep, it's time to go to the gym parking lot. It was kind of empty for a Wednesday.

I took about half an hour to do some yoga poses and to stretch. I needed a spa day which should include a deep muscle tissue message. After the stretching, I walked and let the sun wash my face. I love the sun. I was alive with a bunch of hope surging through my body.

I wanted to finish the book, The Other Wes Moore.

The book store was quiet, and I found a nice table for two and lost all sense of time. Today, I was in the mood for fish and broccoli with some lemon rice and beans and a tall glass of water. Yes, that is what I will enjoy indeed. My fridge is ready to accommodate the request. It was off to Kroger to cash my check. As soon as I arrived, it started to pour out rain in abundance. That is exactly how my life will be, abundant and flowing over.

I reached out to my sister-in-law to see how she was doing and to find out what life in Nevada would be like. I cracked the window to let some of the sound of the rain come in and fell asleep. When I woke up, the rain had died down. I cashed my check and put away my tithe. I am blessed and grateful to have a job. I am blessed and grateful to know that I would be provided for in Nevada. I am blessed and grateful to know that God gave me everything I would need.

As I was getting ready to leave, a young lady selling a variety of homemade products approached me. We spoke about many things including life events, God, her current situation and the direction of her "next". I gave her some money, introduced her to the Victory Church Atl app and told her let the Holy Spirit guide her to the message He knew she needed.

After that, I was on the way to Walmart to get the immediate items only. It's time to start using out the can goods and other items and let the pantry go dry. Preparation for my next had begun. It was time for Access. The most wonderful part of my week was gathering with these like-minded people to uphold, encourage, hug and cover each other in prayers. I love the Pastor, the First lady, the leaders and the volunteers that make up Victory Church Atl. It's the type of ministry that gives you a sense of purpose and helps you put God first in all areas of your life.

You can grow under this leadership. I listened to the leaders as they shared their heart and I received the words of encouragement and heard their concern. I am grateful to be surrounded by these people.

At the hotel parking all the spots, and I mean every parking spot, was gone. To be honest, I did not want to stay there tonight. I headed to a different location and parked, but I could not get comfortable no matter how hard I tried. Then, I drove right back to the hotel parking lot and there was a spot that was opened up. It was facing the street. I was more in view than ever before, but it was where I was supposed to be.

Dozing off and jumping up. Dozing off and jumping up. Dozing off and jumping up. It was 11:30 and I was tired. Every noise caused me to jump up and look around.

I was getting to high alert status where the gorilla would take over and that beast ain't pretty.

Then I heard a still small voice say, "I am with you."

Well, on that note, I put on the gospel of Matthew, lay on the pillow and had a great night's rest while I slept.

Thursday August 25th

I slept until 4:30. Thank God for helping me sleep.

All around me was still. When I slept, it was trusting that God would keep me safe and He did. I cannot do what God is capable of doing and He does it well I should add.

It's time for part one of the morning routine, then it was time to leave and head to Kroger. I spent just a moment longer on washing myself because I want to enjoy the soap bubbles for just another moment. I was aware that it was a public bathroom, but I still wanted to enjoy a private moment under the circumstances.

I headed for gas, hot water and ice. I have no desire to linger this morning, so off to the gym parking lot I went. It is time for stretching and personal development.

As I was sitting in the car, a pickup truck came by, drove around the car and parked by me. A young man came out and approached me. He was short and stocky and Asian and stood his ground with authority. He said, "I always see you out here, are you ok? Do you need help?" All I did was smile. God sent an angel to check up on me.

His name was Peter and he had a story to tell. I told him all was well, and I thanked him for being brave enough to approach me. He told me his testimony of his walk with God. He shared his heart about his youth, what he likes to do, coming into a relationship with God, being a servant, serving in a church as a teacher, having his own computer business, the joys and pain of marriage and the importance of security.

I listen more than I spoke. He was full and flowing over. I was more conservative with what I shared with him because I felt that there is more he wanted to say but was feeling me out. I asked him one question and it was simply, "What does the word minister mean to you?" He told me his thoughts that were very intimate and personal. He spoke from his heart and I was quiet. After he was finished, I simply said "Peter, to me, minister is to attend to the need of someone. It is to serve. You are ministering to me right now. God knew I was in need of one of his representatives to pour encouragement into me, so he sent you to do just that.

If you reflect back, you will see you have been on assignment for most of your life." He is quiet, the truth was taking root. We held hands and then I prayed with him and for him. I gave him a hug and thanked him for being transparent with me.

We went our separate ways.

I went to the Library and wrote. About 2 hours later, I was on my way to the Mexican restaurant for rice and beans and then I found a cool shaded place to eat. Later that afternoon, I headed to my brother and sister-in-law's home to spend time with them and the 4 kids. My nephew came out to greet me. "Aunty Michele check this out, I can touch the rim!" He then proceeded to show me what he can do. He did indeed touch the rim. I was the proudest aunt.

We spoke about school, life, church and sports. He helped me take my things inside and then joined his father, Jermaine and Roland in putting together the entertainment unit. My nephew is truly a gentleman. That night we had a good family dinner and then it was time to tell them that I would be leaving Georgia to go to Nevada.

Each child processed the news of me leaving their own way. There was a mixture of disappointment, questions and hugs. I respected their space.

That night, Lena, Krystal, Alora and I had a cup of tea and some grown folk conversation. It was a great time. We talked about marriage, dating, how they met the men that would become their husbands, attraction in marriage, relationship with God, knowing what battles to fight and how not to let your better half disturb your peace.

It was a great round table conversation that was so good we lost track of time.

I took a hot shower and crashed on the couch.

It was a sweet sleep.

Friday August 26th

I woke up to hear the kids getting ready for school. It was a beautiful sound.

There were small footsteps running down the steps, breakfast, early morning chatter over cereal and milk, voices getting ready to head to the car. My youngest niece came by and gave me a kiss on my forehead and said, "I love you Aunty Michele," and I opened my eyes just in time to see a backpack turn the corner.

The house returned to being quiet. I slept until 7:45. Usually at 7:45 I am in the gym parking lot stretching, so to be resting felt somewhat odd. I missed having a bed. I missed having a fridge. I missed the convenience of hot or cold water and the simple pleasure of throwing myself on a couch. I took a hot shower and washed my hair.

After getting dressed, I went with Lena to drop my nephew off to school. We spoke about the kid's progress in school, the sense of independence that the oldest was coming into, building confident kids, teaching accountability and responsibility, giving the older ones more freedom in certain areas of their life, this next upcoming move of my life, expectations and so many other things.

By the time we returned, the household was coming to life. There were "good mornings" and movement and breakfast and coffee and hot water and eggs and stuff like that. I drifted away to put my thoughts on paper. Soon it was time to go. They were on the way to Ikea, but I did not want to take the chance with the Atlanta traffic since I had to go to work.

I gave them each a hug and headed to the book store instead.

I ate and got some rest. It was soon time for work. I saw a young lady whose face I recognized. It was my sister, Mary, and I was happy to see her. She was in the neighborhood and wanted to drop by to share a smile. I truly love my sister. We chatted and then, it was time for her to hit the road. I gave her the ultimate hug and she left. I headed inside and greeted my co-workers.

The store manager stated how much he would miss my positive attitude. That is a good thing. He wanted me to help him find a replacement. I agreed and prayed that the right person would be led to the store just like I was. My immediate manager was distant. I said hello and got right to work. It was Friday, and we were busy.

After work, I headed to Barnes and Noble to unwind.

Some hot water with honey will do nicely. It was time to get the night clothes together, prepare the clothes and toiletries for tomorrow, and make sure my water was in place. It was time to head to the hotel parking lot. I found a good spot and parked. There is someone in the car besides me. We nodded to each other and continued to ignore each other.

I saw another spot that was better, so I pulled out and drove into the new spot that was closer to the front. I finished setting up, adjusted myself.

I asked God to watch over me and I fell asleep.

Saturday August 27th

God I am alive. I am safe. I am yours.

Thank you, Jesus, for another day. It's 4:30am on a Saturday. In about 2 more weeks, I will be stepping out to another phase of my life, but while I am here, I will praise the Lord.

I started the first part of the morning routine and then left the parking lot to get to the second part. The morning was quiet. "Self, remember its Saturday so, no lingering." I appreciated my reminder and did my part. Upon leaving Kroger, I greeted the usual faces, and then off to the Quick Mart gas station for the needed items. Usually I would go to the gym parking lot but today, I headed to the Home Depot parking lot.

I re-twisted my hair then cleaned up my car inside and out. It was time for the library and some phone calls from the parking lot. I called other close family members and informed them of my decision. Today, I prayed for the man that will be my husband. I don't know who he is or where we will meet, but I prayed for him. I prayed that the favor of God would be on him, safety for where ever he currently is, for God's love to be wrapped around him, that he would love himself, that he would love God and that he is somewhere praying for me. I told God I am looking forward to meeting him.

Where did that come from? That had never happened before.

After the library, I went to get some grub and then it was off to work. The store manager was in high spirits and we conversed at the door. My immediate manager had more to say to me today. I hoped that whatever she was dealing with that she would find strength.

Today, I spent the time tagging items and printing out price tickets and making sure all the newer items were prepared for delivery to the sales floor.

It is a very busy Saturday and soon it was over. I had tuna and a biscuit and some hot tea while I decompressed at the bookstore. Then it was time to head to the hotel parking lot. There were 2 spots to choose from, so I went into both to see what felt better.

I would not spend tonight being uncertain or concerned about anything.

I set up my bed and went to the back seat. I prayed for myself and others who are in the same situation.

I put my life in God's hand and thanked Him.

It was a quiet night.

Sunday August 28th

Well Lord, one more week to go. Its 2:31am.

One more week and I will be finished with work and start to prepare for more. I have been praying for a safe plane ride. Its 4:37 am. The parking lot is actually busy this morning. Lots of folks are leaving early to start their journeys. I brushed, flossed, scrubbed and washed and sat back for a moment. "This is about to come to an end. The next will begin in 2 weeks. Actually, the next has already begun; this process is the bridge that I am crossing," I said to myself. That's how I am looking at it at 4 something in the morning.

I headed to the grocery store.

The bathroom was dirty. I cleaned it and got my morning duties started. Then, I headed for ice and hot water. While inside the gas mart, Mr. Harlan and I spoke for the first time. We spoke about the goodness of the Lord, how He is kind beyond words, His ways are not like our ways and sometimes the best lessons are on the other side of the worst experience. I thanked him for being so in tune and sharing his heart with me.

It spoke to my situation and to my hope.

Today, I will treat myself to a fulfilling breakfast. Something that all of me will love when I eat it. "Self, what do we want to eat today?" I asked. Lately I had begun to look deeply into my eyes, looking to see what? Looking to see whom? I'm looking because there are two perspectives I am witnessing. Oh well, I'll figure it out later. "You know what; today will also be a good day. Before I go to work, I am speaking a positive experience with my co-workers, the customers, the managers and whoever else strolls through the door, amen," I prayed. The atmosphere was still. This Sunday morning is already a blessing.

Sunday is busy at work. We had a lot of suits that came in and they had to be unboxed and tagged. My coworker came by to share his heart with me. He had arrived at the point of his relationship where he was no longer mentally satisfied. That's a tough one because when it comes to matters of the heart, one must proceed with caution.

Whatever decision he makes, I pray that he does not let pity or manipulation control his emotions. I pray that his frustration does not lead to potential abuse, even if it's subtitle. I pray he understands that no woman wants to be with a man that tolerates her.

After work, we spoke some more, and we prayed for guidance for him.

I went to get the needed items and head to the hotel parking lot. There's a great spot that is waiting for me.

Yes, look at God.

The night was quiet, my mind was quiet, and my smile came from a quiet place.

I looked up at the roof.

"I'm gonna make it, I'm gonna make it," I said silently.

Monday August 29th

Man listen, when you wake up and your hip is in pain, you know it is time for your next.

"Lord I am thankful. I am assessing the past and I am thankful. I am assessing the present and I am thankful. I am in serious pain and I am thankful. I am one day closer, I am thankful. I am alive, and I am loved by you, I am thankful," I prayed.

My morning responsibilities were taken care of. My stretch routine and yoga was well needed. My hip appreciated it. I did not walk today. It's Monday so its laundry day. I listened to my personal development while folding my clothes.

It would be a long day at work, so I decided to get it started early. I had a conversation with the GM. I wanted to share some ideas that could better the place. He listened out of consideration.

I had this overwhelming pull to share my heart with my co-worker. It is very transparent and energizing. It's amazing how someone's need can be met at the right time, with the right words to help usher someone into their next. I was grateful that I would be considered to be used for His glory.

There are lots of boxes and packages that kept coming. There was no time for too much chit chat. I blinked, and it was after 3. Then blinked again and it was time for home. I headed to the book store parking lot and took inventory of everything. I was living the life of a minimalists.

By the time I headed to the hotel parking lot, all the good spots were gone and I am in a spot that had me feeling exposed.

I could not sleep so I went inside to the hotel lobby to unwind and think. The chair was comfortable, and I enjoyed some Ramen noodle soup. Strolling back to the car I noticed an 18-wheeler that was towards the end of the parking lot that is sitting idle.

I am protected.

Tuesday August 30th

Its 2:27am and I can't go back to sleep.

I am edgy. Dozing and up. Dozing and up. I did not like the fact that I wanted to sleep but can't. No matter what position I would turn in, I couldn't find sleep. I am sleepy, but I am alert. I turn on the bible app and listened to the gospel of John.

I slid down to my knees and crouched as low as I could and folded up as tight as I could. I don't know why, but it felt like this position is what I am supposed to be in. A few minutes later there was a bright light that shined in the car besides mine. The light was so bright it lit up everything inside my car, and then it shined 3 cars down from mine. Jesus. Had I been asleep, I would have been seen. "Lord I am thankful for your care and your commitment to my safety, thank you." I prayed.

The police car drove off and I was still on the front carpet. Since I am down here, I might as well get on my knees and that's exactly what I did. After my prayers, I sat in the front seat and looked out the window. My mind was on caffeine and sleeping pills both at the same time. I was about to complain when I heard the small voice, "If you can't sleep it's because you insist on watching out for yourself instead of letting it sink in that you are being watched over."

Well, I guess I have been chin checked. Again. I'm just going to sip some tea, roll over and find my position and sleep.

The mornings were beginning to be a blur as I was on auto pilot. As I was in the middle of the routine at the gas station, it hit me. Michele, your father has given you the fortitude to survive anything, even this. I smiled to myself and my confidence tank increased that moment. I thanked my Abba and my Father, who are both in heaven taking care of their daughter. I have been guided and protected, led to different places, kept safe and have been getting more and more understanding about my life and God's value in my life.

I have no reason to complain. None.

Frustration had caused me to be agitated but grace had caused me to be humbled when I saw the "why" behind the agitation. And so in my being stripped for greater, I have learned that agitation is a catalyst that is used to prod me from complacency.

As I drove to the book store, I felt these words, season, release, faithfulness and tangible. Man, these words had me on a high.

I praised God while I was driving. I am sure that the other drivers must have thought I was crazy.

As I arrived at the parking lot of the bookstore, I had to write with a sense of urgency the following thought, "I feel it in the atmosphere, this is only for the faithful, for those who held on to the word of God, for those who said to themselves, though he slay me, yet will I trust Him. For those who said, Lord I can't see the whole picture, but I trust you during the process, for those who sacrificed even when you were insulted for doing so. I have a strong feeling that there is a release. This release will be tangible. You will touch it, you will see it. It will be a quick turnaround. It's as if there was a test, and the faithful passed." I received this for myself also.

It is time for work and man is work waiting for me.

There are boxes of the remnants of summer shoes and fall shoes. It is the type of day that keeps one occupied and engaged until it's over. "One day closer Michele, one day closer."

After getting what is needed, it was time for the hotel parking lot. There were a few spots that were scattered about. I went to all of them to see what felt right.

None of them did, but I did not complain.

"God don't sleep, I do," and off to sleep I went.

Wednesday August 31st

Its 5:00am, exactly 5:00am.

I slept for 5 hours straight. Usually by this time, I would be at the Kroger and in the bathroom. I sat in the car feeling somewhat confused and not knowing what to do. A part of me wanted to go back to sleep and a part of me recognized that the schedule was tossed off. It's best to not go back to sleep. I headed to the Kroger and handled the responsibility of my mornings.

I was in the mood to unwind while I ate, so I headed back to the hotel. I strolled into the lobby and headed for the breakfast buffet. They were serving biscuits, cheese and gravy with pineapple, strawberry and papaya. On the way out, I spoke to some soldiers and thanked them for their sacrifice. They were getting ready to drive out and head to their destinations.

As I walked, there were three of them in front of me.

I watched them as they were in one accord with each other. Conversation flowed easily, laughter flowed easily, they had on the same fatigues, the same type of boots, had their gear rolled and ready. They walked with an air of authority and not hostility.

I would think twice before I attempted to engage in anything physical with any of them.

I wonder if that is what those who call themselves "soldiers in the army of the Lord" look like.

After my stretching, walking, personal development, reading and writing time, I drove to cash my check at Kroger and then headed to the mall. It had been a long time since I strolled in the mall. I went to the sneaker store and tried on some old-school Pumas, Adidas and Nikes. I went to get some shower gel to make me smell girly. I looked at all the clothes that were being offered in many of the stores and realized that none of the styles reflected the me I desired to be.

After the mall I headed to a West Indian restaurant to get some food and then decided not to spend any money. I pulled into the movie parking lot and opened my fridge and the food pantry. I ate what I had and that was good enough. I stayed within the neighborhood and that was good enough.

The day became the evening and the evening became the night.

The prime spots were once again taken, and I ended up in the parking spot that made me very visible.

"Dang and Oh well," I said and into the hotel I went to marinated and use the computer.

I took my time to leave and headed to the car.

After setting up the blanket and pillow and sheet, I put on the book of Psalms, leaned the front seat back and went to sleep.

THE CHARIOT

Thursday September 1st

It's September. It's the month of September.

It has been eight weeks that I have been in this mobile home. Its 4:00am and good morning, God. I looked around. The neighborhood is very quiet. The streets are very quiet. Its only 4:00am, but I would rather start my routine early than late.

Driving to Kroger, I listened to the book of Psalms. It felt like it was feeding my soul. Today I will fast until 12:00pm. Instead of the gym and bookstore, I headed to the Costco parking lot and decompressed. I was not in the mood for much of anything today except listening to the Psalms. About 2 hours later, I headed to the cemetery where my father is buried. It has been a long time since I visited his grave site. I cleaned up around the area and went inside to inquire about floral arrangements.

I am here to talk to my father.

I know his spirit is in heaven and this is the place where his body was laid to rest, but out of respect I came to share my heart with him. I updated him about everything. I told him about my mindset, the promise land experience, homelessness, the new location of the church, his grandkids and their new school. I talked about leaving the first job and the reason why, how the current second job was taking its toll on me, getting ready to leave and head to Nevada, hopes, dreams, apologies, praying and wondering about my friends. A lot came pouring out. It was exactly what was needed.

I had to say goodbye to my father, so I thanked him for everything he has taught me. I had my father for 42 years of my life. I never had to wonder who I looked like, or whose temperament I have or what a man is supposed to be or how a man is supposed to treat his wife or how a father is supposed to be towards his children. I never ever, EVER, wondered if I am loved. I know I can do, be and become the greatest me because of what he did for me. He was there.

He was a father.

He was there at my beginning and I was there at his transition. Towards the end of his life, he fought cancer bravely. I saw what applied faith looked like.

He was the beat of my heart and will always be.

While talking to my father, I saw a caterpillar. It was walking and stumbling and tumbling over the grass as it headed towards its destination. It was fighting its way through, onward and around an item. The grass was hot, the weather was hot. The caterpillar rolled and flipped and went left and went right and made its way to the taller grass. As I watched the caterpillar, a movement caught my eye. When I focused, it was a butterfly, a yellow butterfly that made its way from the right side of the trees to the left, but what happened next caused my jaw to drop.

As I followed the path of the yellow butterfly, a beautiful multicolored butterfly left the leaf of the tree and flew straight towards me. It was eye level and kept coming towards me. I wanted to move but my feet were stuck, and I was in its path. I am in awe of what was sent to represent the beauty of my next in the now. It kept flying towards me.

Then as it came within arms distance, it flew directly over my head. My eyes and my head tilted up to watch it as it flew over my head the way one would watch an airplane. What an awesome wonder. The butterfly kept going on its merry way. I could not move. My mind tried to wrap itself around what I just experienced; my feet were glued to the earth. "That's you, from a caterpillar to a butterfly, go to your future," I thought.

I smiled because that was indeed me. Self, that is indeed us. A visual representation of what just happen in the supernatural. I got my release and I am not wasting any time. I am leaving Georgia with a clear mind. This one is for me.

There is a future I desire to have that is stuck behind what I don't understand, but as I am going through this current process, it is helping me to value the intangible things more and more.

I prayed and thanked my father for all he had said, the example he showed and the sacrifices he made. I thank my father God for every breath I took and every protection and provision that came to me through His Grace and Mercy. I thanked Jesus for the privilege I have to call on His name and the power of His blood.

This season was the beginning of God engraving himself into my heart and solidifying himself as the air I breathe. My issue of un-belief and lack of trust never stood in God's way of taking care of me. It stood in my way of surrendering to Him, but even with that, He looked past my faults and saw my need.

I received my father's blessing. Everything he taught me was engraved in my heart. He would live there until God calls me home. I read my father's favorite Psalm to him and ended with a prayer.

As I was about to leave I saw a worker sitting under a tree trying his best to keep cool. I drove by but then had an unction in my spirit to go back and offer him some cold water from my fridge. I drove back and offered him some and his face lit up. We called over his co-worker and I gave them the cold water. They were grateful and exhaled loudly after the first drop hit the back of their throats. I know the feeling. I said my goodbye and headed to the library.

I read Luke chapter 17 earlier in the morning and it mentioned the lepers and how one came back to give thanks. I went back to give thanks to my dad. I gave thanks to my Kingdom Father also. I am now fully ready to transition to Nevada.

I headed to the other side of town to get some fast food and to take care of my financial responsibilities. Then I headed to the gas station. In my haste, I drove off without pumping the gas and then I returned. The attendant mentioned she noticed I left and was kind enough to allow me to get the gas. I went to spend time with my brother and sister- in- law and the kids.

I had grown folk conversation with them, read a bed time story to the two younger ones, took a hot shower and slept in a bed.

Today was a good day.

Friday September 2nd

I tossed through the night. I was not used to sleeping on the bed.

I woke up, went with Lena and Philip to drop the kids to school. Then I saw something that made my heart smile. My nephew, who is 11 years old, came out the vehicle, and ran up to the school door and he opened the door for a girl that was about to go inside the school. After she went inside he went in. Man listen, that touched my heart and it touched his parent's hearts also. He is such a gentleman. He has a large presence.

After morning conversation, I did my morning routine, got dressed and received an envelope from them on the way out. They blessed me with what came from their hearts and it was appreciated. As I started the car, I became concerned. I headed to the local neighborhood car wash and I saw my good friend Robert. I vacuumed the car and cleaned it out really good. My friend gave me a free car wash. He is so nice. He will be a great father and husband one day.

As I sat in the car and began to go through the car wash, I began to reminisce about all the people I have met in the last 8 weeks.

So many people that were sent into my life to seek my interest. They gave with no strings attached. It's hard to not see the beauty of God in them. In every encounter, in every word, in every prayer and in every favor, they extended me. Even in the events that were not so pleasant, there was still the goodness of God.

I came out the car and wiped away the water and the car looked crisp and clean. I hugged and thanked Robert for his kindness since the day we met. He thanked me for helping to point him back to Jesus. I think my father, both of them, would be proud of me. We prayed and said our goodbyes.

I headed back to the book store and decompressed. It would soon be time for work. Upon my arrival, my immediate manager gave me words of encouragement and a hug. It was appreciated. My co-workers were positive, and the environment was light. The shoe department was busy. I did well with commissions.

After a satisfying day at work. I headed to the bookstore for hot water and lemon. I drove around looking for a new parking spot, but I knew I was just wasting my gas so off to the hotel parking lot I went. The prime spots were gone and only the ones in the back were available.

My mind was already focused on the next. Ever since the visit to my father's grave site and that experience, I am more at ease with my next.

The windows were cracked.

The night air was definitely cooler, and I loved my life.

Saturday September 3rd

It's 3:13 am. Still tired. I rolled over sank deeper under the sheet.

Its 4:37am. This is as late as I will sleep. The morning routine was calling and since it was Saturday, I would not risk trying to fall back to sleep.

After my morning routines, I decided to head to Walmart to get some needed items. Today I wanted soup for breakfast. There is one cashier, there are 12 people standing in the line at 6:15 in the morning and the self-checkout section is closed. Why Walmart, Why? There was soon a lot of grumblings and agitations that began to rise from the customers. People began to abandon their items and walk away with a few choice words. I left also.

The local gas station was quiet. It usually is on a Saturday. I got my hot water and my soup and went back to the hotel. As I drove the check engine light came on and I was concerned. I did not include anything for car repairs in my budget. I prayed and ask for heavenly intervention, "Lord, keep my car until I leave. Protect me as I drive and extend grace to the performance and integrity of the car, in Jesus name, amen".

I am considering taking up jogging. I was told that it tends to bring clarity and that there is something called "the second wind" that kicks in when you think you have reached your limit.

This would be the last week that I would be scheduled to work and for that reason I had a very heavy schedule. I walked to the parking lot and sat in the car. I need to write, and then sleep.

The work day was busy. The end of summer sale brought in the crowds and the time kept ticking away. People shopped for shoes, sundresses, Sunday apparel, suits, shirts, jeans, ties etc. I helped a family shop and as I walked them outside to their car, we held hands and prayed in the parking lot.

Some of my co-workers gave me hugs and words of encouragement as they left, "just in case I miss you on Monday," they said. I really liked where I was.

Perhaps I liked it more because I was leaving.

After work, I stayed in the parking lot. I did not feel like going home. "Home, what home? A public domain that any and all types of people pass through as they go elsewhere? Is that what you have the nerve to call home? You don't have a home and because of you, I don't have a home".

Whoa! Where did that come from?

I don't blame the gorilla, there are many times I wanted to get away from myself, but I always seem to be around me. I definitely have to learn to jog so I can release.

I went for a drive. For about 30 minutes I drove aimlessly. I don't know if I was subconsciously looking for a new spot or simply in need of running away. I should have left for Nevada earlier. Restlessness was pushing me to get going. Why exactly had I stayed this long in Georgia? I'm not worried. The time to leave was closer than before, and I was more than happy to leave. I always felt the West Coast pulling me, especially California.

I drove back to the hotel and parked. The front seat was not comfortable. The back seat was not comfortable. Sitting up was not comfortable nor crouching down was comfortable. Walking around the car was not comfortable. I was just in one of them type of moods. I turned on the bible gateway app and listen to Genesis. "In the beginning..." The beginning sounded like a great place to start.

What type of a different beginning will I have in Nevada? Will it be the type of beginning that will bring an end or prepare me to begin again?

Finally, I settled down in the passenger side of the car.

I pulled the sheet over myself and leaned the chair back as far as it could go.

I am looking forward to my new beginning.

Sunday September 4th

Its 4:39am. It's Sunday, I want to sleep longer.

It's usually slow on Sunday. I mean, most people will not be getting up early to go to the grocery. I felt a nudge in my spirit that said, "If it ain't broke, don't fix it". And on that note, I will stick with the pattern and not break it.

It was quiet at Kroger. It was quiet at the gas station. It was quiet in the gym parking lot. I decided to go back to the hotel and marinate in the lobby. I enjoyed a light fruit breakfast and packed away some biscuits for later. I lingered longer than usual and watched as the lobby began to come alive with visitors passing through. I had this strange feeling to go back to the gas stop so I did. While there, I saw a young lady with her hood up.

She needed a jump and unfortunately, I did not have the cables to assist her. "Perhaps I should buy some coke. I heard a bottle of coke can jump start a car," she said. While I was encouraging her not to do that, a police officer pulled up. I approached him on her behalf and at the same time another gentleman asked if he could be of assistance. I left her in good hands and drove away.

I headed back to the gym parking lot and decided to get my regular morning walk and stretch in. I noticed that my clothes are fitting more loosely. My weight is dropping. I am eating to survive. Fact is all of me is in survivor mode. I listened to the Sunday message entitled, "Be Set Free." I rededicated my life to Jesus Christ. I asked him to give me stamina and strength to keep pushing. In my weakness, His strength was what I needed.

I did not push myself today. My body, especially my hips were not in the mood to be aggravated. I decided to take it slow. My co-worker decided to share her heart with me. The more she spoke the more I realize that the reason I was led to this job was because of her. I had servant work to do and it was all because of her.

My life is not my own, my assignment was over.

That afternoon, I was approached by the GM. I was accused of something that was not true. I told him that his accusation and cynicism was on a false basis and he was wrong. He did not want to accept what was said so we argued back and forth. In the end, I told him straight to his face, "It's my character that you are talking about, if I were you, I would be careful." I think the calm manner in which I said it caused him to think twice before he responded.

The gorilla encouraged me to keep getting riled up, but I cannot let her have her way. I waited, and when my manager became quiet, I walked away.

I left at 7:00pm and gave my co-worker a hug. He was my favorite. We exchange numbers and promised to keep in touch.

I headed to spend time with my nieces and nephews.

We had family movie night and talked some more.

When the kids went to sleep the grown folks had their time.

Soon and very soon.

Monday September 5th

The house is quiet. I am thankful for the night's rest.

I take care of morning responsibilities early out of pattern and habit. As I was getting dressed, I noticed a shadow at the bottom of the door. I opened it to look into the face of my 4-year-old nephew who was soon joined by my 6 year old niece. They wanted cereal and milk for breakfast. I sat and watched them as they ate and had young people conversation over breakfast.

As the house began to wake up, I made my way out the door. I gave everyone a hug and hit the bricks. The sooner I could get to work, the sooner the day would be over. I had a 10-hour work day and to be honest, I did not mind at all.

I spoke with Ms. Lawanda and we shared our hearts about many things. I gave her the last piece of my plant because I knew she would take great care of him. His name was Buster. We also spoke with another co-worker, Daniel, who said he received a job offer and would too be gone soon.

I told him how proud I was of him and he gave me the most monstrous hug. He said I inspired him to push forward. He said, "Ms. Michele, don't let anyone steal your joy." I received that from him.

We talked some more and imparted words of hope and encouragement into each other. I was sent there as a servant for him also. He gave another monster hug and we went to our different sections of the store to help the customers. He will be a great husband and father someday.

It was Labor Day, and the first part of the morning was slow. I organized, talked to customers, laughed with co-workers and made sure I got work done and in place for the manager for tomorrow. I got many hugs from some of the regular customers. I truly loved the way the day was ending. At the end of the night, the GM blessed me with some items as a going away gift. We had our moments, but we had respect for each other.

We spoke in his office and he gave me words of encouragement. I truly appreciated the fact that he took a chance on me. We hugged, and I left his office. I walked around my area to make sure everything was in great condition for the next day.

When I was satisfied, I looked around the store one more time then left.

This would be the last night I would sleep in the car in the hotel parking lot on the street. I drove around the parking lot and found a great spot. I prepared for the night.

I decided to sleep on the front driver's side and stretched out.

I was too excited to sleep. This would be the last night it would be like this, the last. I listened to Deuteronomy, one of my favorite Old Testament books.

Moses truly was one heck of a leader.

It was a good night's sleep.

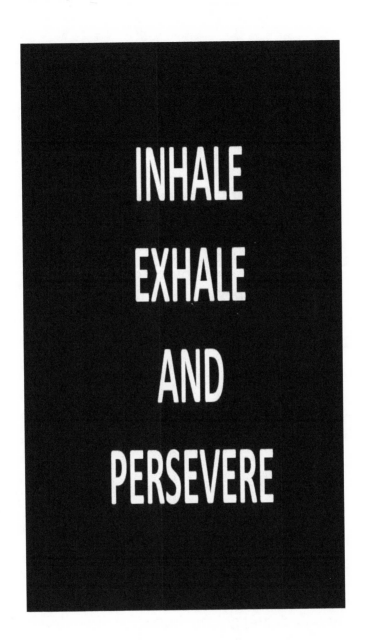

Tuesday September 6th

I am usually an early riser and today was no different.

Today, I looked in the mirror and reminded myself that this would be it. Today, this day would be the day that marked the beginning of the end. I thanked God for the season He walked me through. After I took care of my responsibilities, I headed to the gas station and was greeted, "Good morning Ms. Ice and Hot water." They always made me smile, and I thanked them for that kindness. I stayed outside a little while longer and cleaned out the car.

Today was going to be a great day.

I decided to go to the hotel and get some breakfast. I had 2 English muffins, 1 boiled egg and some fruit. I was then off to the gym parking lot for deep stretching, yoga and personal development. It was time to pack and thin out my minimalist wardrobe even more so off to the storage I went.

This storage that was once my place to come and take a "water bottle shower" was now the place I would pack and get my items for travel together. The time was slowly arriving quickly. By the time I put away, repack, and told myself, "I don't need this in the desert, this can go for donations, I have definitely outgrown this particular item, I better hold on to this just in case," it was 3 hours later.

Lunch today would be rice and beans with tuna fish and cold water. I had to go to my job to get some items out of lay-a-way. After I paid for everything, I said my goodbyes. I drove to some of the familiar places that helped me get through this season. I parked in the parking lot and inhaled and exhaled. "Wow God, look at how far you have come with me, actually look at how far I have come with you, thank you".

I headed to the other side of town and spent the evening with Philip and Lena and the kids. The house was alive with noise and laughter and running up and down stairs and "stop it" and "gimme it, it's mine" and "stop Joey" and "Oh please, you don't know what you talking about" and "Aunty Michele, can you help me" and all the life that comes with having 4 vibrant children.

I don't know how parents do the routine day in and day out. I truly believe that one must have a calling on their life to be a parent because my God, it is hard work!

Wednesday September 7th

I hear the footsteps of younger children.

It's time to rise and shine. I took care of morning duties and then went into the kitchen to say hello to everyone. Lena and I took the first group to school. We prayed on the way for their safety and for the safety of everyone in the school from the smallest to the eldest.

We prayed for them to have a great day of learning and favor with the teachers. After the drop off, we returned for round two and prayed the same thing for him.

I saw my nephew's mid-semester progress report. He had 100's, 98's and a 91 across the board. Man listen, if I had grades like that in school, my parents would have been doing back flips and summersaults. It was set to be a long day for me. Even though I was no longer going to work, I did have lots of little things to do and must get it done.

I took items to our ministry office to retrieve it later, had to make arrangement for the car, get to the pawn shop to take out items and get them into storage, just lots of back and forth. I went to get something to eat.

However instead of eating at the restaurant, I had a notion and decided to eat in a shady spot towards the front of the parking lot.

There was an older lady that sat in her car and was decompressing. After I ate, it was time to clean out the car and get rid of items. The pantry was very bare except for 3 packs of tuna fish, some crackers and a can of beans. The fridge was bare except for 3 cold bottled waters, the last swish of almond milk, yogurt and a can of soda.

Everything cold was placed into 2 garbage bags with the last of the ice. Everything pantry related was placed into a Walmart shopping bag. I looked in the direction of the car and decided to give the older woman the yogurt. As I walked over, I asked her if it was ok for me to bless her with my yogurt. She accepted it.

Man, when I looked at her she looked preserved by God Himself. Her skin was clean and smooth, her hair was grey and well-kept, and her clothes were classy. After I placed the yogurt in her hand, I felt in my spirit I should pray. I asked her if it was ok for us to do that and she agreed. After we prayed she looked me square in my eyes and said, "Young lady, I felt that prayer. What is your name?"

Usually I don't give people my name when I am sent to do His work, but I felt the need to honor her. "My name is Michele".

"I Am Grace."

BAM!

My mouth opened, and my eyes widened. I was stuck looking at her. I was struck looking at her. I was speechless looking at one of Gods characteristics in the flesh. A characteristic that was my constant companion since this episode began and throughout all my life. I was speechless looking at Him through her as He visited me. He came and sent a reminder of what had helped me keep my mind. He sent a reminder of what had protected me. He sent a reminder that I was not forgotten. He sent a reminder to remind me to never forget. He came to show me He loved me.

In this season of being stripped for greater and in this personal visit from an angel on assignment, it finally sunk in. I finally understood the magnitude of God's love towards me, His love for me and His commitment towards me. Because I personally experienced His generosity and His kindness, it fulfilled my life's deepest desire.

I started to fall deeper in love with God.

Thoughts swam in my head. She was silent. She nodded, winked at me, got back in her car and drove away.

I don't know how long I stood there, but somehow, I had wandered back to my car and was simply leaning against it. I could not move.

It was Wednesday and soon it would be time for Access. I headed to the job to get my check, and then off to Kroger to cash it. As I was about to pull out of the Kroger parking lot, a car just came out of a blind spot speeding to get to where it had to go. I hit the brakes. The car beeped its horn and kept going. I continued to drive toward the DMV and arrived at the light. The light changed to green, but I had a feeling to just sit still for a moment. A car that sped up to beat the red light kept coming and ran right through his red light. Jesus!

Then as I drove, I had to turn off of the main road to get to the DMV. I started to turn and the oncoming 4x4 ran his red light and kept right on going. My God! What the what! I arrived at the DMV safely and just sat and inhaled and exhaled deeply.

Grace.

I spoke with a sister that was very professional with great customer service skills. As I made arrangements for the license plate, I ask her if she was ok. She said he was going through. I asked her if I could pray with her and for her and she said it's what she needed. After we prayed, she thanked me for being obedient to the Holy Spirit and came by today.

It was time to get the car into the appropriate persons hand and we met at my old apt complex. I prayed over the car. I thank God for keeping it together just for me. I prayed it would take care of the next owner as it took care of me. I cleaned it up and vacuumed it and put some cotton candy car fresher in it. I watched it as it left me. I felt a little sad because we had history.

I walked to the hotel that I once drove to. I sat in the lobby with the other guest and looked out the window. Life was ending and beginning. Life was happening in this hotel to every guest. One guest was talking loud with much masculine bravado of accomplishments. Another guest was scrolling on her phone. A married couple was looking at each other.

Another guest had just arrived into the hotel and was at the front desk checking in. Younger children were on their electronic devices. I felt like I was watching a movie, participating and observing both at the same time.

It was time to head to Access. My prayer was one of thankfulness. Some folks I hugged, some folks I laid my hands on their shoulder and squeezed as a sign to encourage them. We prayed for those who would be the next semester of small groups (V-Group) leaders and then everyone prayed over me for safe travel, protection and provision for whatever would be next for me in Nevada.

After prayers, I got my items from earlier and headed up to spend a couple of days with my sister. We arrived safely. After we decompressed it was time for "grown folk conversation".

I love my family for real.

Thursday September 8th

Its 9:00am. I slept until 9:00am

I walked around her home and smiled. I am so proud of her. She has come a long way. I went into the bathroom and looked in the mirror.

I was in a state of rush, but I had to be reminded that I am not on the street. I slowed down. I took a hot shower. Luxury is in the simplicity of a moment you appreciate. I came out the shower and got myself together. I had to remind myself that I was not on the street. As I got comfortable, I wrote and then listened to Proverbs 15. Then it was time to stretch and read.

I received a text that agitated me. I decided to wait until later to answer it, I knew if I responded, it would insult the person and cut them deeply. I would wait. Then I read Proverbs 15 again and there was my answer in verse 1. "A soft answer turneth away wrath, but grievous words stir up anger." (KJV)

After reading and listening to Proverbs yet again, I ask God to help me compose the text. I responded to the text in a manner that shocked even me. Usually I would put the person in their place. Instead, I was instructed to respond to answer from gratefulness.

I went for a walk and admired the neighborhood. I came back into the apartment, stood on the balcony and enjoyed the view. I enjoyed the moment of being there.

The day came and went. I was restless being inside. I was so used to being in certain places at certain times that I was restless being still. I wanted to be out and about but I also wanted to start coming down from my experience. I don't know how long it would take.

Eventually, evening fell and I cooked some food. I actually cooked some food. On the stove, with pots, going into and out of a real fridge that had fresh ingredients. When she came home, she greeted me and went into her room to unwind. After she came out we ate and had more "grown folk conversation".

I slept but did not rest.

Friday September 9th

Its 6 in the morning.

By this time, I would have already taking care of all the morning routines and heading to the gas station. I would be sitting in the car taking a moment before making my way inside for ice and hot water.

Its 6 in the morning and I am enjoying a cup of hot lemon water with honey while looking over the balcony. I don't know how long I was there, but I heard my sister say she was leaving to go to work.

After my morning routines were taken care of, I went for a walk. The neighborhood is very progressive. There is a lot of movement. Cars constantly in motion. People constantly in motion. Very active. After strolling for a few, I made my way back to the apt.

I watched a movie named Black Hawk Down. It engraved itself into my senses. I sat on the balcony for only God knows how long. When she arrived home, we headed out for seafood.

It was a night of good food, double twisting of the hair, laughter and appreciation.

I totally love and value my sister Mary.

Saturday September 10th

Its 6:00am. I feel the need to read and write.

The day was busy for us both. She took care of her responsibilities and while she was gone, I wrote and listened to some Jazz. Upon her return, we headed out to take care of the little things, shopping, nails, eyebrows, groceries and all the bits and pieces that one does on Saturdays.

"Soon Meesh."

"Soon indeed."

It's Saturday.

It's almost that time.

MY
AUTHENTIC
VOICE

THE FOUNDATION

BROTHERS AND SISTERS AND UNCLES AND AUNTS

Sunday September 11th

This date takes me back to when the Twin Towers were attacked in New York, but on this day, this date took me forward to worship and fellowship with my brethren.

Its 7:32am. I have been jumping up since 3:42am. Perhaps it's from the days of sleeping in the car, but fact is it is from the excitement of knowing that today, Victory Church Atl has a new location to worship and praise God in. New area to bring the gospel to, new and familiar faces to fellowship with, the same radical Jesus loving, vibrant group of folks who love to worship and praise God but will be doing it at a new location.

I'm fired up and ready to go. We pack all our items and they are sitting by the door. All of my ministry obligations have been successfully transferred over and place in the capable hands of Sekou, Jermaine, Kia, Mama E and Nikia.

I have no worries.

Today, I will receive. I am going to praise God with such fierce urgency that the intensity might set someone's soul on fire. "It's time to go Meesh." We hit the door with enthusiasm in abundance.

My mom drove from a long distance to spend time with us. It was good to see her. The Experience was awesome. Pastor spoke about faith. He referenced Luke 22 starting at verse 31. Man listen, the prayers that Jesus prayed for Simon Peter was that his faith may not fail. He never prayed that Simon Peter would not go through. Instead he prayed that when he goes through, his faith would be there to keep him strong. Every word Pastor spoke described my situation. That message was tailor-made and handcrafted for me and no one else.

After all the announcements, he mentioned that I was leaving and there was a feeling of disappointment from many. I received prayers, hugs and words of encouragement, tears and some also blessed me with finances. Being with this fellowship of believers has given me so much courage and matured me in my walk of faith.

They helped me accept accountability and responsibility and to grow in so many different areas of my life. I truly love and value them.

After church the family gathered to eat, talk, watched movies, laugh and fellowship.

At about 2:00am, I was awakened by my family due to some concerns that they had. They wanted to make sure that I was fully aware of possible differences, of understanding my expectations, of making sure I had weighed the pros and the cons of my decisions. "Meesh, are you sure?"

I am so loved by these brave and beautiful people. My brother Philip, sister-in-law Lena and my mother. I know the magnitude of their love. I value the years of contributions in so many different ways and the words of guidance.

I give them the assurance that reaches their ears that I am at peace. I could see in their eyes that in their hearts, they are not.

I am so sorry for that lack of comfort.

I pray for their comfort and peace to come.

Somewhere deep within, there is agitation that must be confronted so it can be removed or better understood. The time had arrived for me to come forward, but there is something that is holding me back.

The time had come for "it", whatever "it" was to come out of hiding.

I had to get some questions answered.

There are some "whys" that are clawing at my soul.

I am going on a journey to get my answer.

THE TRANSITION FLIGHT CREW

Monday September 12th

THIS IS IT!!!!

My eyes were opened. Thank you, God.

It's Monday September 12th and I am about to take a 2,221.4 mile journey to get some answers. I am up early and antsy. I get myself together, spent time with the kids at breakfast and took the car ride with them as they went to school. After praying for them and for all the teachers and parents and other children, they said their goodbyes and were off to learn. This was part 1.

Upon our arrival home, I spoke with my family and thanked each one of them for the early morning conversations, concerns, warnings and wisdom. It was soon time to take the ride for part 2 to school and off we went. My mom prayed and soon my nephew was off to learn.

It was time for my mother to leave. It would be an 8 hour drive with traffic give or take. It was emotional. "If you need anything, you call," she said. "I will. And you do the same," I replied.

I love her so much.

It would soon be my turn. It was hard for me, but it was necessary. After making adjustments to my suitcase, it was time to head to the airport. I appreciated the quality time with all of them. After we said our goodbyes, the reality of the decision I made had just sunk in. "Man, I am really doing this thing," I said to myself. I went through the process of shoes coming off, walking through the metal detector, scanned and screened and all that was necessary for me to have a safe fight.

"Damn right pulling that one to the side. He looks suspect for sure. Thank you TSA". That ain't right gorilla, that ain't right.

It was my first time on Southwest. As I boarded, I asked the flight attendant if I could get a picture with her, the pilot and co-pilot when we landed safely. She smiled, welcomed me aboard and said, "yes of course." The flight was full. As I walked towards my assigned seat, all I heard was, "I can't wait to get to Vegas" or "It's my first time heading to Vegas" and "No sleep till Vegas." I know the feeling.

I sat on the plane by a window seat. As I looked out the window, I was in a place of uncertainty and discomfort. All that was fear, all that was hostile, all that was the deepest part of my anxiousness began to surface. My mind was on high alert, the gorilla was threating to come out and fight somebody on the plane, all kinds of notions about dying in the desert after surviving the plane crash was trying to start a riot in my subconscious. I inhaled deeply and exhaled slowly.

"Michele, what the fuck are you doing? You just packed up and left everything and everyone based on your brothers word? You have not seen him for 28 years. You don't know who the fuck he is or what he does or nothing. He could be some shady, grimy dude that when he see you will be disappointed in who you are or how far you have not come. He could have played you like a sucker. What if he's crazy? What if he invited you out to Nevada and then forget your ass and now you in the airport. You going all the way Nevada to be homeless and look like a fool." These were my thoughts.

What if, what if, what if. No! "Peace be still!"

I know that God did not bring me this far in my faith for me to be forgotten or overlooked. "He won't fail me. My brother will not fail me," I said to myself.

It was time to fasten the seat belt and get ready. We began to taxi down the runway. The speed began to increase and soon we lifted off. The feeling of my guts being weightless and doing 2 back flips both at the same time began to bring a smile to my face. "It's official. I made it."

The passengers on the plane were rowdy and loud. Conversations included pulling an all-nighter in the casino, which hotel gave better comps, after the conference who was going where, memories of Old Las Vegas, the prices of food, visiting that hotel that had the dancing water fountain that they saw in the Oceans 11 movie and the excitement and promise of walking the whole strip from one end to the next.

For them it was about the bright lights and the experience of Las Vegas, for me, it was excitement and anticipation for the next chapter of my life, my time, my next. Nevada held my next. I was on the way to meet my brother, his wife, their friends, their life and my next.

I have no idea who any of them are, and they have no idea who I am.

The flight was great. The scenery began to change as I looked out the window. There were lush images of green that slowly began to thin out and eventually became what looked like a sea of brown sand. So many shades of brown, beautiful to behold, dangerous to be in without experience. "I am going to touch that. I want to know the feel of desert sand raining off my fingertips," I thought.

I applauded when we touched down. I totally loved the pilot and had to meet the people who helped us arrived safely. I waited until the crowd thinned and was the last to leave the plane. True to her word, I did get my selfie with the flight attendant, the captain and the co-captain.

As I gathered my bags, I looked at all I had. I came with 2 suit cases, my purse and my faith. I came on the word of my brother. I traveled what is equivalent to about 2,221 miles on the word of my brother. "I did it. I actually did it. This can't be real. Am I really in Vegas? Wait, let me find the Welcome to Las Vegas sign. I got to do a selfie. I got to pinch myself and savor this moment, and maybe get something to eat, but first, let me get a selfie." Click! It's official now.

I walked through McCarran International Airport feeling some type of wonderful.

Stepping out on faith is nerve wracking but on the other side of pushing past fear is the ultimate satisfaction of knowing.

Wait, wait. Is that a slot machine in the airport? Vegas baby...Vegas.

And there he was. OH MY GOD. It's HIM!!! OH MY GOD. It is my older brother from my biological mother side. Anton. I felt like a groupie, but it's him. In that moment, I was transported back to Trinidad, West Indies. I was 4 years old and he was about 5 or 6. We were playing outside at the side of the house. He had a white t-shirt, red shorts, black rubber boots with white around the top, and a make shift red cape. "I'm spider man watch me," he shouted and with much exuberance, fortitude, effort and perseverance, he climbed up what was the giant brick wall that separated the neighbors from us. I total fell in love with him that day. My brother was indeed spider man. When he came down the wall I looked at him and became his biggest fan. "See told you I could do it!"

I could not move for a moment.

And then I went to him. After a monster hug, I stepped back to study him. He is tall. I think he is about maybe 6'1 and round. He reminded me of an image of Buddha when I saw him. He wore white linen and had prayer beads around his neck. His hair was salt and pepper. Age and experience had engraved itself onto and into his face. His eyes looked like it had seen life. Rough life, pleasant life, ups and downs of life, what the hell am I doing in this situation again, life. He was the most beautiful thing in the airport. I wanted to cry. The joy in my heart was so much it was painful, but a smile that was brighter than Las Vegas showed up instead.

We walked outside and I met a young man and for the sake of his anonymity, I will call him John. My brother said, "Sis this is John and he is my family." John gave me the most awesome of hugs. It was therapeutic. I wondered if he knew that. I was so glad to meet him. He's the type of guy you could take to TGI Fridays and have a good meal and great conversation and exchange ideas and agree to disagree and hear great stories from. He looked deeper than he lets on and very attentive. He will be a great husband one day. If he is not already.

As we drove, my brother spoke about the place I would be staying. He said it's a nice place that I would love. "Just think of this area as the Beverly Hills of Nevada," he added. As we drove through the community, I looked out the window and saw rock formations, sediments and sand. OH MY GOD, we are in the desert. No. What? Wait. I am in the desert. Like this is a real desert. No wait.

You don't understand, I am in, this place is in, I will be living in a community that has been carved out as a place to live, by a developer, that decided that in the middle of this desert, homes should go here and hotels should go there and shopping should go there and town homes should go there and a roads should go here and a manmade lake should be put there.

I am in the flippin' desert. Is that a palm tree, placed in the desert, in the flipping desert, by a developer that had a vision to cultivate a community in the middle of a wide open spacious dry climate?

I tuned back in to try to listen to what my brother was saying, but I was in the desert. Give me a moment as I wrap my mind around this fact.

We arrived at a gated community and drove through to a home that was waiting for me. As I came out the car, I paused to look at the neighborhood, it felt safe. VERY SAFE. I walked into the doors of a welcoming home. There was a young man who welcomed me with a beautifully displayed floral arrangement. I stopped to smell the flowers. I inhaled it deeply. The atmosphere in the home was clean. I was blown away by the thoughtfulness of the gesture.

Down the steps walked my brother's wife, Ms. K. She was welcoming, kind and smart. I built rapport with her and was glad to finally meet her. She gave me a tour of the home. It was breath taking.

After things were settled, I headed to the home of my brother and his wife. It was a top floor penthouse apartment. I was given a tour of their home and it was overwhelming. What I loved most about their home, was the view. I could sit on that balcony for hours and just get lost in the view. The view allowed my thoughts to sink in. One view overlooked a lush green golf course. Across from the golf course were other homes, and miles behind those homes were the mountainous sediment of the desert.

There were so many different colors to these sediments, black, dark brown, golden cover and hews of corral and cream. Oh my God I was looking at the most beautiful thing my eyes had seen in a long time. The natural beauty of Henderson, Nevada had engraved itself into me. I felt a pull towards those mountainous-sized sediment rocks. It called me by name. I want to climb one of those. I want to do so much.

The view from the other side of the rooftop pent house was of the community. Looking straight cross the other roof tops, in the middle of what looked like a manmade lake, was a house that that sat all by its self. It was perched on a rock in the middle of the lake and looked lonesome. As if it was in need of attention and appreciation. It reminded me of myself. I looked up and saw a cloudless blue sky. I closed my eyes and felt the heat of the sun; the atmosphere was hot, but not humid or sticky.

The view of the sun, the waves of the lake, the stillness of the house in the middle of that lake, the quietness of the neighborhood, I could hear myself think. It was so quiet; I was straining to hear the noise of everyday life. At least the everyday life I was used to. The hustle and bustle of surviving life. The, I have to get to this place by this time to do this specific thing, life, the car honking, bus driving by, police siren, loud laughter, life. But, this is everyday life, its everyday life that I have not been exposed to at this level with this magnitude of intentionally away from distractions, life.

This was my brother's life that he and his wife had opened up and graciously extended an invitation for me to participate in and heal, life. This was not my normal, this was far from common, and this was the other side of scratching and surviving. This was the after. After all the sacrificing and hard work and crossing the "t's" and dotting the "I's" and making mistakes and finally hitting your stride and doing what you were purposed to do and excelling at it and it yielding major dividends, life.

Their life was DEFINITELY not in any way shape or form AT ALL like my struggling ass life.

But yet he did struggle, he did fall, he did fail, he did make major and minor mistakes. He is on the opposite side of his "I once was".

How? How? How? How? How? How? How?

He must have sensed the question because he gave me the answer.

"Sis, practice till you get it right, then practice some more till you can't get it wrong." It would be the opening line of what would become a 2-3 hour conversation.

I called my family to let them know I had arrived safely and then continued the conversation with my brother. The conversation was seasoned with so many things from our past. We had the same biological mother but not the same father.

I saw him when I was about 5 or 6 and then he was gone. I remember I sat at the door waiting for him. He did not return. I remember looking out the window and asking when is he going to come back.

I waited for Spiderman, but he was gone.

We would connect later in life when I was about 16. He was part of a band and I had the chance to hear his band perform at his high school. He was really good and had high hopes for the band. Then life pulled us on our own paths.

And here I am, at age 46 years old, looking into the eyes of my child hood hero. My brother, Anton. Man I love this dude. I engraved his face into my heart. He had so much to tell and was very engaging. The last thing I told him about was my homelessness.

He was quiet for a moment, then he said, "Life occurs in a larger context," and looked away somewhere in his mind as if some question was answered. It was as if some moment finally made perfect sense.

I went to another home and met a man.

For the sake of protecting his anonymity, I will call him Paul. "You look just like your mother," he said and gave me a hug. He made me a welcome to Nevada home cook meal.

I love home cook meals.

The table was set as if a very important guest was arriving. Gold forks and knives and a beautifully carved branch like center piece and classy crystal glasses and cloth napkins. There were gold goblets to enjoy some wine or water or any beverage and neatly pressed cloth napkins and also the view of the community.

Beyond the community were the mountains and those sedimentary rocks. I was fixated on those mountainous sedimentary rocks. They were all around and insisted on never letting me forget it.

This set up, dropped my jaw. My fist meal was Salmon with shredded broccoli with potatoes and white wine. DAMN!!! The first bite was worthy of me dancing on the table. Oh Shit!!! My mouth had an orgasm and my eyes rolled into the back of my head and I exhaled from deep within my diaphragm. In my mind the gorilla said, "This is some good shit, eat slow, just in case there would be no more."

I was still in survivor mode. I had not unwound; I had not detoxed.

As I sat around the table. I was looking into the faces of Anton, Ms. K, John and Paul. Each of them has their own testimony. They would refer to it as being on a hero's journey. They told of the different life events that had occurred, choices, yesterdays and eventually how they ended up here in Henderson, Nevada and how they function as a family unit. It was a journey like onto mine. It's as if the blueprint was the same but the individual experience was the only difference.

"Life occurs in a larger context," Anton said and asked me to share my story. I shared many things including being homeless, the feeling of being stuck, early mornings routines, night time routines, $.06 cents in the bank and $5 in my purse. My life. My testimony. Parts of my journey. They all stopped and looked at each other. I ate and then looked at them. "That's why," said John. "Now it all makes sense."

"We have been preparing that house for a reason. We decided to open back the Winter House and started to prepare for something that was coming; now it all makes sense. I told K to start getting the house prepared earlier in the year. I did not even know why because personally I don't even like the house, but she got on it and we did our part. We were preparing that house for you.

That house is for you to stay in. It was never for us, it was always for you."

I stopped eating to let that sink in.

"I was the larger context? All the bits and pieces were coming together. That while I was in the state of Georgia, living on an $8.50 an hour 20 hours per week job, sleeping in a car and being covered by Grace and Mercy, God was moving pieces into place over 2,221 miles away. It was all just to bring me into a home worth more than half a million dollars? Me? It was all to put me in a gated community that was the second safest place to live in America? Me? It was all to have me in a neighborhood that was so quiet I could hear myself think? Me? It was all to put me around the most beautiful view of what His hands had crafted? Me? It was all to put me on the hearts of these four individuals that would be seeking my interest. Me?"

I looked into the eyes of these four individuals and said, "Who are you people?" They were quiet. "What the fuck you got us into now, Michele?" The gorilla within said.

There were so many testimonies of Grace and Mercy around that table.

Grace is the most important ingredient that anyone who has been through anything and came out the other side with their right mind would ever come to value. God's Grace and His Mercy.

When voices told me, "I am wasting my time and everyone else's, just take your life and save everyone the expense of your existence here on earth," Grace kept me. When I felt like an embarrassment to myself and my family, Grace comforted me. When I have tried and failed and tried and fail and tried and fail, Grace pushed me. When I cannot get anything right and continue to feel as if something is all wrong. Grace endured.

I am convinced that Grace is favor and hope mixed with oxygen and peace.

My heart was grateful. This place was greater, these people were greater, this neighborhood was greater, this meal was greater, and their commitment to helping me grow was greater. The greater was about Gods love being shown to me in so many different ways, by so many different people along the way in different seasons of my life, using what God gave them, to contribute toward my life.

I had been stripped for greater, and the greater was to love, appreciate, value and honor people as they are and accept them at their level of presentation. It's the intangible growth that the lessons were producing in my mind and heart that was the greater.

All the other tangible items, the things, were simply the icing on the cake.

Ms. K drove me to the Winter House and she shared insight about my brother and our mother. After conversing in the kitchen, I headed up to the bedroom. It was a long day. Within hours I went from the east coast to the west coast. From heat and humidity to heat. From green trees to different colored sand. From rice and beans with tuna and soda to salmon, broccoli, potatoes and white wine. From plastic forks and knives to gold forks and knives and from a car that was my shelter and my bedroom to a 3 bedroom, 1 bonus room, 3 full and 1 half bathrooms, 4248 sqft, half a million dollar home in a beautiful gated community.

"Is this real?" I continued to ask myself.

I am overwhelmed. My chest hurts. My eyes hurt. My senses are being bombarded. I want to run. I can't breathe. I sat at the edge of the bed, and watched my 2 suit cases. Ready. Just ready.   Inhale Michele. Exhale Michele. Breathe Michele. Just Breathe.

The shower was hot, the bed was comfortable. I tried to stretch out on the bed but it felt foreign to me. I laid on top of the comforter on my side, curled into a fetal position and covered with my sheet with my head on a strange pillow. I thought about my life.

A life that I was, for the most part, grateful for, but never satisfied with. There were splinters, dark corners, unresolved issues, broken self-made promises and dissatisfaction with emotional relationships. There were sexual abuse, abandonment issues, feelings of inadequacy, and self-inflicted agony because of my thoughts, decisions and emotions that were reactive.

I am toxic. I am functioning...broken.

I thought about my family, my mother, brother, sister-in-law, nieces, nephews and my sister. I thought about all my nieces and nephews that range from age 4-31. I thought about all my brothers and sisters scattered in different cities, living life. I thought about, Durham, NC, the church I served in faithfully for 11 years, the variety of jobs I had and my college days. I thought about Georgia. I did not like living in Georgia. It was a painful event that bought me to Georgia.

I thought about the variety of businesses that failed, the lack of personal commitment to my own self and my dreams, the open doors and favors that photography had given me, the variety of people whose hands I shook, the thousands of images I had taken as a photographer.

I thought about Victory Church Atl, the church I had served in faithfully for 4 years.

I thought about the different areas of the ministry I was privileged to serve in. I thought about the people I had served with and the lives that were changing because of the Gospel of Jesus Christ. I thought about so many faces and hugs and just the caliber of the people.

They were far from perfect but committed to persevere.

And finally, I thought about my father. The reason why I left everything, and moved to Georgia in the first place. He had cancer and was fighting the brave fight but he required more. As a family, we rallied tighter to care for him, and he was worth every sacrifice that could be made for one person. The night that he died, my mother and I were around his bed reading him his favorite psalm when he exhaled loudly and went home to be with God. My father was the beat of my heart and when he died, my reason for doing and being died. He was in my life for 42 years, 42. He was the most stable and steady person I had ever known. He was the most positive and motivating force in my life. The most!

I grieved for 18 months.

The only thing that kept me sane during that time was going to church, serving in the ministry and my family. It would take me 18 months to come to understand that we, as a family, had buried my father, but I had never laid him to rest. I am so sorry for where I am in my life. As his daughter and for all he poured into me, my life did not accurately reflect what I could do or all he and my mother did for me.

The quiet night, in this Henderson, Nevada neighborhood had me facing hidden truths, buried truths, painful truths.

I did not qualify nor did I earn this place where I currently physically am.

No. I was considered.

I was at the beginning stages of being humbled, there was more to learn, it's why I am here. There is something or someone I must face. There are some things I must come to terms with and some losing to bear. I feel it deep within my feminine intuition. My stripping for greater has only just begun. There is greater confrontation, greater understanding, greater appreciation, greater release, greater value, greater relationship with self, people and God.

Greater has a price.

As I drifted off to sleep I heard the door open. My brother walked in, kissed me on the cheek, walked out and closed the door.

I fell asleep.

MY MORNING VIEW

Tuesday September 13th

I was in a car.

I slept in a car, with leather seats, in the Georgia heat, covered with a sheet, lying on top of a blanket with a pillow under my head. The windows cracked for air to come in at night from July until September 2016. Sweat was my constant companion by day and by night, an occasional spider was my visitor, four doors were my entrance and my exit, the trunk was my kitchen and my closet, a Styrofoam cooler was my "fridge", and a plastic container was my "food pantry".

Bottles of water were my shower head and plastic bags were my bath tub. Irish Spring was my summer fragrance, bathrooms at a variety of locations that had a lock were my private place. Calgon could not take me away; the reality of my decisions had brought me to a place where I could not even look into my own eyes. It was more than shame, it was disappointment. That was the self-inflicted wound-- disappointment.

I am now in a house that was set aside for me. A house 16 miles southeast of Las Vegas. I am in the second largest city in Nevada. In 2011 this city was ranked America's second-safest city.

This city has been named one of the best cities to live in America. Arriving to this location had the most interesting mix of gradually changing scenes. This landscape consists of deserts, large mountainous sediments, the most beautiful clear sky with no clouds and a variety of shades of the sand.

I looked out the window and the view made my breath get caught in my throat. My mouth fell open. The neighborhood, the quiet, the sun as it began to cast its rays on the mountains. I saw it change the mountain to the most beautiful golden hue of good morning I had ever witnessed with my own eyes.

Is it possible to fall in love with a mountain?

I sat up in bed and checked the time. I was late, but late for what? That sense of surviving had come to an end. I did not have to hustle to get anywhere by a certain time. "It's the bed's fault that we are late; it's too damn comfortable." The gorilla was not used to her routine being broken. I was not going to entertain her today.

I prayed and read the bible at a leisurely pace. I was led to read Deuteronomy chapter 8. I read this chapter and had to read it again. Did God just speak to me directly? Let me sit still and let this soak in because for a moment I thought I saw myself in the bible again. That can't be. I must really be mentally fatigued because for a moment I thought I saw what was my current situation clearly laid out for me to see, right there in the bible again. Is it possible that different chapters of my life's events have already been written out, tucked in the bible and I am simply seeing and reading about myself as I am living out my life?

"This is too deep this early in the morning. Did I come all the way out in the desert to be this deep this early in the morning? No this thought is too deep this early in the morning. I simply want to watch the mountain change its shade as the sand reflects the sun rays." I stood by the window and watched the beauty of all that is natural respond to all that is High.

I went into the bathroom. A bathroom that I was told was mine to use. The towels were fluffy, the bath mat was fluffy, the washcloths were fluffy and all the amenities of toiletries were already provided. I did not want for anything. Ms. K knows how to do her thing. I saw my reflection in the mirror. I was small. My eyes were sunk deep into my head and there were deeper dark circles under my eyes. I know how I usually looked, and man, I looked tired.

Life events had taken a toll on me.

I went from a size 12 to a size 8 and weight under 130 lbs. I was healthy but had been through. I wanted to crawl back to bed and sleep but old habits kept me from doing just that, not to mention that there is a 3 hour difference in time zones so technically what the time really is, it isn't, but it really is.

I liked the color scheme of the bathroom. I turned on the water and let it run then got in. I turned the water as hot as my skin could take it. I am taking a desert shower. I know it's under the roof of a home, but the home is part of a community that was built in the desert. Just as Las Vegas has bright lights, hotels and life, well that life is happening on a strip that was carved out in the midst of the desert. "You know what, I'm thinking too hard on this thing. Really I am." I stayed under the hot water, used a rag with a great smelling gel, and lathered up all my nooks and crannies. "Yasssss, oh my God Yasssss."

When I came out the shower, I stood naked and flossed and brushed my teeth.

I wiped some of the steam off the mirror and could only see clearly for a moment. It was enough for me to catch a glimpse of myself. I need to take better care of myself. After I dried off, I put on lotion that smelled like cocoa butter. I dressed in a skirt and a loose blouse. I felt like a girl. I felt feminine.

I went into the fridge and could not decide what to have for breakfast. I closed the fridge and then opened it again. Then closed it and then opened it again. I decided to have bread with butter and cheese, with hot water and lemon.

I sat on a bar stool type seat and ate in the kitchen. The house was quiet. It was me alone there. The kitchen was by far my favorite place in the house because of the richness of the color of the granite counter tops. I can sit here all day with a block of sharp cheddar cheese, a sharp knife, unsalted crackers and hot lemon water and just marvel at the kitchen while I eat.

I walked up the stairs and marveled at the stair case.

The crafting on the wood was beautiful. I actually wanted to get a can of pledge and bring out more of the beauty of the wood. It was a deep mahogany brown that played off the tightly woven carpet made for high traffic area. As I reached the top of the stairs, there was an oval window that afforded a view of outside.

Natural light bounced off the wooden table-like cabinet that held a most beautiful bowl that drew the eye to the moldings in the window. Whoever built this house took time to invest into this house being a home. I walked by slowly to absorb the light and peeked across the street to see clearly into the neighbor's home. They also had a window that allowed in natural light.

I felt a strong need to write.

I retrieved my tattered notebook. It has been my companion that held the quiet thoughts of my daily life. On my way down the stairs, I allowed my hands to hold the staircase with more appreciation. I walked through the kitchen and slid open the glass sliding doors and stepped out into a marvelous light.

A wonderfully well laid out back yard with grill and summer furniture and trees and leaves and shrubbery and desert stones and a water fountain that was waiting to be used when needed.

I found a spot, sat my behind down and was lost in writing my thoughts for 2 hours. I closed my eyes and lifted my face to the desert sun. I loved this place. I love the environment of this place. I loved the silence of this place. I loved the low humidity of this place. I knew I wanted to stay in this part of Nevada for as long as God would let me. There was healing for my soul here.

I exhaled from my womb.

I wondered who my brother was. I wondered about his core. Did he love Jesus? Did he know Jesus? Did he believe in God? Other than our biological mother and childhood memories, what else did we have in common? I knew he was smart. No actually he was more than smart, he was a certifiable genius. His mind was off the flippin charts.

My brother was the type of person that if you left him on the corner of any Main Street in America and came back within a year, he would own the whole neighborhood and would be strategically making plans to go after the next town.

As I sat on the outdoor furniture I ask myself honest questions. "Michele why did you come here? What do you hope to find here? What do you hope to let go of here? What is here for you that is not in Georgia? Did you run from Georgia or did you leave Georgia? Is it yourself you are looking for? Are you sure you are here? Who are you Michele Nicole Mitchell and what makes you think your brother can help you find yourself?"

In the morning sun, in the quietest of neighborhoods, under the most beautiful blue cloudless sky I have ever seen, I explained to myself the reason why I am in Nevada. "There are answers he has. There are things he knows. There is life he has lived and places he has been and experiences he has endured and he knows more about our past than anyone. I came to see my brother with my own eyes and touch his face and see his smile and spend quality time.

To ask about our past, get some healing from my past, understand my present and get some personal development. My past. Who is our mother? Who is our grandmother? Where did I come from?

What is our lineage? What are her demons? Are they mine also? Why is it that there are things I do that have been taught and there are things I do that are from a place that is naturally within me that when it acts out I cannot explain? Why did her leaving hurt me so deeply? What am I longing for? Why still long for it all these years later? Anton, what the fuck is wrong with your sister?"

That is why I am in Nevada.

As I sat under the sun, in the desert, I reached for my phone and looked at the notes I took from a conversation we had months prior. These are the questions he asked me. "Are you ready? Are you willing to allow the transformation? Are you willing to allow yourself to change? Even if it takes you to a place you don't like and a place you don't understand? The dark places that are within you, are you willing to go through the process?

Are you ready to find the true you?"

I left it all.

I left everyone and everything because I want to find me. Me. This journey was not for anyone else but for me. This one I had to do it alone and learn to trust me.

My voice is in this desert, my courage is in this desert, my health is in this desert, the higher performing me is in this desert. The decision maker is in this desert. My freedom is in this desert. I traveled 2,221 miles to face something in this desert.

There is life in this desert.

I sat under the sun, in the back yard of a house, in a community that was built in the desert.

It would be in this quiet neighborhood that I would meet the most dangerous thing known to man.

And it would cost me my blindness.

THE DESERT

ACKNOWLEDGEMENTS

For my family, friends, the different people who have been assigned to me on my life's journey, the Victory Church Atl ecclesia and the strangers who have been "angels on assignment" when it was needed:

I truly thank you all from the bottom of my heart.

I am especially grateful for my Abba and my Father. Both are in heaven looking down upon me and encourage me daily to stay the course.

"Dad, I am making use of your bible."

Michele Nicole Mitchell

DEFINITIONS

Strip: Remove all coverings from; leave bare of accessories or fittings; to deprive of possessions, office, rank, privileges, or honors.

Agony: Extreme or intense physical or mental suffering; the final stages of a difficult or painful death.

Sabotage: Deliberately destroy, damage, or obstruct (something); any undermining of a cause or activity.

Agitate: To move or force into violent, irregular action; to upset; disturb; to be troubled emotionally and deeply.

Traumatize: Subject to lasting shock as a result of an emotionally disturbing experience or physical injury.

Fortitude: Courage in pain or adversity; mental and emotional strength in facing difficulty, adversity, danger or temptation courageously; emotional power or reserve and ability to withstand.

Circumcise: To cut off the foreskin (of a young boy or man, especially as a baby) as a religious rite; to purify spiritually.

Desert: A dry, barren area of land, especially one covered with sand, that is characteristically desolate, waterless, and without vegetation.

Know: Have developed a relationship with (someone) through meeting and spending time with them; be familiar with; to be aware of something as fact or truth; to perceive directly; to have understanding of; to have experience of.

LET US CONNECT

If you are interested in inviting Michele Nicole to your conference or to participate in a roundtable discussions, she can be reached at michelenicolemitchell@gmail.com

Michele Nicole Mitchell

@michelenmitchel

Michele Nicole Mitchell

Stripped For Greater Book Review

Professional Review by Jerome Tripp

★★★☆☆

TITLE: Stripped for Greater

Author: Michele Nicole

GENRE: Thematic Autobiography

Personal Overview:
I am honored to had been chosen to edit and review your work! Your story was enlightening and provide me with a small window into a segment of your journey.

Review:
Stripped for Greater is a non-fiction thematic autobiography that chronicles the tough experiences of Michele Nicole in her homeless experience on the streets of Atlanta, GA. Michele depicts her experience as a religious rite of passage that was designed to elevate her on a higher spiritual level. Michele brings a personal, introspective lens on the challenging and sometimes mundane day to day activities of living out her car, bathing in public restrooms and having breakfast at various continental servings at local hotels. In her time surviving as a homeless woman, Michele journeys

through various self-revelatory lessons that she would learn about herself and her relationship with God.

The theme that Michele announces through various points of her journey is that being homeless was God stripping her of her dependence on everything so that He could teach her how to depend on him. In additional, the greater represents the place that God would take her into after her time being homeless. Although the theme is present in the story, I'd like to see the story lead to "greater works" as depicted by scripture for the Christian walk. Though we share with Christ in his sufferings, we also shall reign with Him as well, according to Christian doctrine. I think Stripped for Greater would deliver a much stronger purpose if the "Greater" was tied to a much more powerful destination. Perhaps to achieve this, more recounts of Michele's life after being homeless should be added to the story.

Michele delivers Stripped for Greater in a causal and sometimes comedic voice that allows the reader to understand her persona. You feel as if the story is being told to you over a casual lunch with a friend. The story does well with offering descriptive wording to assist with the experiences Michele faced from day to day while being homeless.

ALSO BY THE AUTHOR:

E-Book, Barnesandnoble.com, Booksamillion.com
and Amazon.com

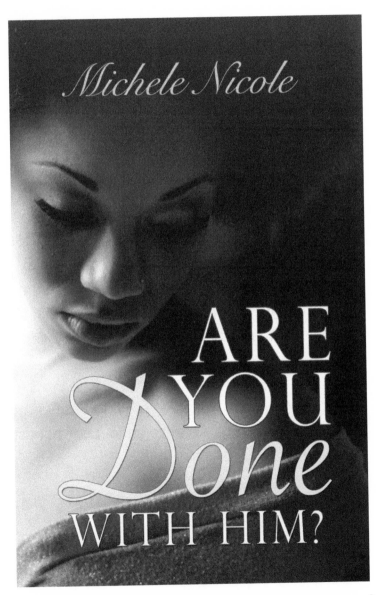

TITLE: Are You Done With Him

Author: Michele Nicole

Reviews:

From: Ms. Karen

"I don't believe I finished reading a book since I was in 5th grade. I wrote on my vision board and on my 30 before 30 list that I would finish a book and I'm proud to say that it was yours.

It was a page turner that I could not put down.

It was real, transparent, engaging, and relatable like you wouldn't believe. You had me going down memory lane with my parallel story. You left me on the cliffhanger though Lol, but I read every single page inside the book and I thoroughly enjoyed it".

From: Ms. Love

"Your book was truly a great read. Put me in touch with emotions I didn't realize I had. Your honesty was amazing".

From: Texas Diva
It's her journey...gotta respect her story

"This is Michele Nicole`s story, the author, of a
destructive relationship and her discovery to get out
of it AND TRY NOT TO REPEAT IT. One may not agree
nor understand why she stayed as long as she did,
endured all that she endured, and once
out...returned, but respect must be given for her
emancipation.
Must keep in mind, when reading, that this is a real
story and who can criticize a person`s true journey? I
would have liked to know more about her after her
self ~ worth discovery, but I enjoyed reading her
story and am sure it can/will help some women
finding themselves in that situation. If open ~ minded
and have respect for a persons trials through
life...this is a difficult (b/c I hate unhealthy choices
endured by any woman) but good read".

From: Shanise
"Pretty good book. It was a great book, enjoyed reading it. Looking for more from this author. Wish it would have been a little bit longer".

From: dwgodby
Challenging Yet Rewarding
"This book by Michele Nicole is based on her own personal experiences she has faced in life. She has written the material to both help herself move forward in life as well as to assist other ladies who find themselves in similar battles. She deals with her feelings, desires and needs which help her to become a better lady after she processes all that has occurred within her life.

She has a close friend MJ that she shares the ups and downs of these life changing events. There is one statement that she shared with MJ in the book that I found very rewarding. She told MJ: "I compromised to be with him." When Michele understood that she made compromising choices to be with this man for three years she began to understand what those choices had caused and what she needed to do to become the person she truly desired to become.

The author leads us through her life describing both the positive as well as the less than positive experiences in life. However, both help to make her the person she is today one who will make wiser decisions to become the person that she truly desires to become.

While I understand this book is based on life experiences and meant to be told as such, however, I personally would have liked for it to used less strong language. I could see the value of the material being used for both personal and group discussion however some would be offended by the language. Also the author talks about being thankful to God and getting her life on track. I would like for her to expound on that and her relationship with God. Maybe this could take on the form of more of a self-help book with discussion questions at the end"?

STORIES BY THE AUTHOR:

Amazon.com

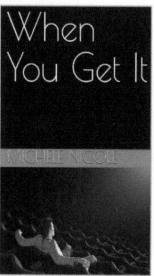

The Cure For My Anxiety

Michele Nicole

Follow
Instructions

Michele Nicole

Still

Of

Use

Michele Nicole

When
Expectations
Disappoint

Michele Nicole

Exhale
With
Gratitude

Michele Nicole

Emotionally
Immature
Manager

Michele Nicole

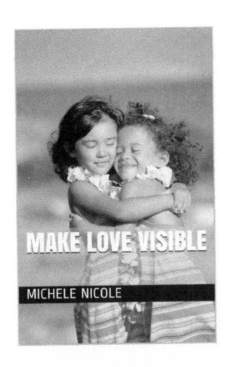

MAKE LOVE VISIBLE

MICHELE NICOLE

Be
BOLD

Michele Nicole

Think About
What
You Are
Thinking About

Michele Nicole

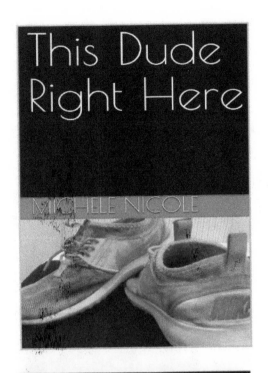

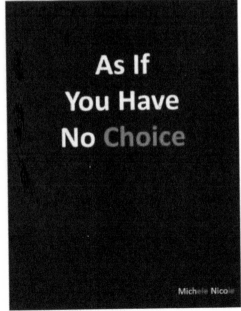

A
Tainted
View

Michele Nicole

A
Perspective
Of
Aloneness

Michele Nicole

The Fear
Attached
To Surrender

Michele Nicole

SPONSORED BY:

Visit Us: www.ShareYourHeart.org

Contact Us: share@shareyourheart.org

Be Inventive In Hospitality

Donate To Share Your Heart, Inc.

$shareyourheart

Share Your Heart, INC

THE ASSIGNMENT

"Simon, Simon, Satan has asked to sift all of you as wheat. But I have prayed for you, Simon, that your faith may not fail. And when you have turned back, strengthen your brothers." -Luke 22:31-32 (NIV)

TRUST IN THE LORD WITH ALL THINE HEART; AND LEAN NOT UNTO THINE OWN UNDERSTANDING

IN ALL THY WAYS ACKNOWLEDGE HIM AND HE SHALL DIRECT THY PATH

CPSIA information can be obtained
at www.ICGtesting.com
Printed in the USA
FSHW012159170219
55736FS